Painting With God

Finding God Within

Adrian Keats

Adrian Keats Publishing House Inc.
Toronto, Ontario
Canada

PAINTING WITH GOD
by Adrian Keats

Published and distributed in Canada by
Adrian Keats Publishing House Inc.:
www.adriankeats.com

Edited by: Carlos Tomas, Catharine Magee,
Christine Zeldin and Nick Caione.

Cover art by: Adrian Keats
Cover design by: Inscapes Creative Print & Design

E-Book ISBN 978-1-7779981-0-3
Paperback ISBN 978-1-7779981-1-0
ISBN 978-1-7779981-2-7

PAINTING WITH GOD
TABLE OF CONTENTS

HEALING LIGHT

I believe it is important to mention the past eight months has been a period of time in my life which forced me to re-evaluate everything about myself and who I am. I experienced unexpected health issues. I've also experienced situations that have made me question the people around me and where I was heading in my life, with my career and with my search to know and find God.

When this year started, I was enthusiastic and excited about so many opportunities that lie ahead. Now, in this moment as I look ahead, I still find there is much to look forward to. However, with the challenges I have faced in the past eight months, I can easily say I have questioned everything about my life and my spirituality - where I've been and what I've done. I've looked with a microscope at my earlier development, intuitively and spiritually, and as I've done so, I've been left with more and more questions as I've evolved this year.

I found myself reaching out to God in ways I never have in past looking for answers and resolve with problems that constantly arose throughout the year. I found my healing abilities internally becoming stronger. I found myself looking to find solutions to problems I never expected I would be facing in past. But this year, I have faced many situations emotionally, spiritually and physically that I was not expecting. Slowly but surely, I came through all of the problems and faced each and every one of them.

There are still many unresolved problems. It has taught me much about patience, understanding and forgiveness with myself and with others. I still searched to know more about the God I always believed, felt and knew beyond a shadow of a doubt was there with me. This year has made me question so many different things about my life and my belief in my guides and God and I think if anything it has given me a deeper understanding and greater love of God.

I think what I would like to say more than anything is I believe in God and God's miracles. Can I fully say that without any doubt whatsoever? No, I cannot. Even though I have seen

Introduction
CREATIVE EXPRESSION

Painting with God evokes an image of many people who are desiring to open themselves up to their creative side and to release all those capabilities they've kept pent up for most of their lives or it's an avenue of giving people permission to access their creative abilities. Painting with God is an avenue that allows people to give themselves permission to express their creative abilities that have been hidden or locked away for a long period of time.

As I painted over a period of two to three years, I started to learn that I was capable of so many other things other than just painting, such as writing, music and singing. So many things came to unfold over time because of painting with God and I found, as I painted with God, I became more and more creative.

Years ago through talking to God and painting with God, I came to realize God was telling me to give myself permission to open up to who I really was. You might open up to who you really are and decide, for example, you want to be a mechanic and decide to open your own garage, take motors apart or fix cars and trucks, whatever it might be.

You don't know what your creative side might lead you to. Creativity is not limited to just painting and writing. Creativity can be design. It can take on so many different forms, don't you think? So as a woman ages, she might find she wants to become a nurse or a lecturer or a therapist and help people. This would be a creative side of her that she learns to express more and feels more fulfilled. Destiny may take her in a whole new direction creatively.

It depends on how you define creativity.

On my journey, creativity is about allowing myself to express the God within me to the fullest.

Dedication

I would like to dedicate this book, Painting with God, to my good friend and business partner, Nick Caione, who made this book possible. He has seen me through the most difficult time in my life in the past eight months and has stood by me when others failed to do so. I respect his courage and strength more than I can put to words and I thank God time and again for giving me such a good friend as a gift for I could not have survived without him.

miracles in my own life and with friends, I still am hesitant at times to believe fully that God will create miracles. I know God can create miracles, I've seen them. I truly believe God can heal others when they least expect it or even myself when I least expect it. I do believe it is possible.

I believe there are people in the world who have these gifts and the gifts are phenomenal. I believe as each of us learn to tap these abilities which we have inwardly, and this is only my personal belief, we all have the ability to heal if we so choose. Yet, I think it takes an incredible amount of work to develop that healing ability over years. It may take two, five or ten years. It depends on how much one is willing to sacrifice and how much one believes.

If you believe strongly in God and in God's healing abilities, then I believe your development might be faster than most. I think and I would hope in the years ahead we all could come together as healers and appreciate the Divine Light within us that God has given us. This is what I believe Atlantis was all about.

When and if all of us lived in the time of Atlantis, I believe spiritually we all had a bright light and that light enabled many of us to be able to heal easily and without many challenges. And this is the road I believe we are back on again which is trying to find that gift to be able to heal with light. Hopefully by the time I pass into spirit in this life, I will have found the light that I am searching for that will heal one easily. That is not to say I want to live forever. I don't. I simply believe we can have exceptional health if we believe and I believe that light within us can grow brighter and brighter with each passing day if we nurture it.

And so, my suggestion to each of you reading this book would be nurture your inner light over time and watch it grow and be thankful and at peace with the gift that God has given you in this life to have a bright light to help you and others to grow and heal in every possible way.

Adrian Keats
November 2021

Chapter One
INSPIRATION WITH GOD

I am beginning to discover
in so many ways
just how miraculous my life is and has been
from day to day and from moment to moment.

I am sharing with you a prayer
you can use in your personal life
if you so desire.

This is my prayer:

> *Dear God,*
> *Thank you*
> *for showing me*
> *all the things that are possible on this miraculous day.*
> *I am sending healing energy to the ones I love.*
> *I am grateful You are always with me,*
> *showing me the way in lighting my path.*
> *And thank You for showing me love*
> *and for blessing those who are in my life.*
> *I appreciate them and love them dearly.*
> *Amen*

How I decided to write 'Painting with God':
The title 'Painting with God' came to me
while painting in my garage, where I almost always paint.
Over time as my art became more and more exquisite and larger and larger,
I began to recognize that when I paint,
God is with me.

God is with me
in every breath I take
and in every stroke,
whether it is with the palate or with the brush,
I am inspired.

And as my life becomes more inspired with each passing day,
this is something I have decided to share with you.

I hope this book inspires you to follow your dreams.
Perhaps you wish to write poetry,
or short stories, or even novels,
or to paint or sketch,
or to travel and seek adventures you've always desired,
whatever that might be.

It could be simple.
It could be complex.
Maybe you have a dream to travel.
My suggestion would be this:
regardless of your circumstances,
choose to make it happen.

I would also like to share an affirmation
I use each morning and throughout the day:

> *'God is with me. I am healing.*
> *I have nothing to fear'.*

As I age, I realize I've spent a good deal of my life in fear,
without consciously knowing I was fearful.

Gradually, over time, I could see
there was a great deal of fear in my life.
Fear is something I desire to lay to rest.
I trust that God will help me to do that
as I look and pray each day
to discover more about myself
and more about others.

The prayer I shared at the start
really is the truth for me.
I appreciate each and every individual in my life.
Everyone who comes and goes are always a part of me
and a part of what I enjoy.

And if I look at the greater picture,
as a part of God,

as a part of a greater family,
we all belong together.
We need to help each other as we go along.

And that is what I would like to speak about:
fulfilling your destiny, your desires,
whatever they may be,
regardless of whether everyone agrees.

No matter how simple or how complex,
you are allowed those desires and those dreams.
God has given them to you for a reason.
You have given them to yourself for a reason.
Take pride in your dreams.
Take pride in the joy and in who you are
and what you desire.

There are no mistakes in this life,
only what we assume to be mistakes.
There is no right.
There is no wrong.
It is what it is
and we learn from each mistake we do.
I am learning as I write this.
I am learning every day.

Am I a good, loving, caring person
to all who I meet?
I cannot say that I am
for I too am limited by my capacity,
my ignorance and my naivety.

I too must learn from my mistakes
and recognize I'm not always right.
I desire to be
but what is right and what is wrong?

It is just my perspective,
or a vision,
or sometimes it's an intuition.

Sometimes it's just my being downright unaware.

Yet, I do not condemn myself in any respect.
I am human,
I am frail,
I've made mistakes
and I will continue to make many mistakes over time
as we all do.

We all wish to correct all of our mistakes.
Some we can.
Some we can't.

Perhaps that is where the sadness is.
We cannot go back
and relive it or redo any of it.
We can only start from where we are now
and live each day better going forward
and live it fuller and richer.

This is what I believe God desires of us.
This is what my connection with God has taught me.
God desires that we live each day to the fullest
and that we live out our dreams
no matter how simple or how complex they may be.

As I move forward,
I am living out my life to the fullest
and to the richest that I possibly can.
I am becoming a better healer
and a better person.
I am fulfilling my destiny
regardless of the fears that I face every day.

I believe COVID-19 ("COVID") has certainly limited
most of us in our capabilities and our desires.
It certainly has challenged us in our abilities
to express who we are, and what we are.

To say I believe that COVID does not exist
would be unwise.
Disease obviously does exist
as a part of this physical reality.
Do we need masks?

Don't we need masks?
Do we need vaccines,
or do we not need vaccines?
These are personal choices.
They are neither right nor wrong.

We make our own choices
to get through each day,
perhaps safer,
or less stressed.
It seems with COVID
and the diseases that confront us,
we may be living more in fear now
than we ever have before.

Fear of the unknown.
Fear that we might be punished
and that death sits at our doorstep daily
enough to frighten some of us about going out.

I'm not sure this is the best way to live
but it is what we have been taught to believe
that death is at our door
and we must be vigilant.

Vigilant for what, I am uncertain.
I do not wish to preach right or wrong.
I do not want to tell others
how to do their jobs
or what we all need to do.
We each must find our own way, our own path
and find what is true for us.

And so, I travel with God.
I am safe.
I do not have to fear because I travel with God.

Does that protect me from COVID?
Does that protect me from disease?
I highly doubt it.
I certainly know one thing
and that is depending on what I've chosen,

I will draw in what I need to learn.

Sometimes sickness does help each of us
to grow and to learn.
Do we choose sickness willingly?
I am not choosing it willingly or consciously
but subconsciously perhaps
I chose to learn something from it.

God has helped me to sculpture my life and to paint it.
God can help you to sculpture your life
and paint it and paint it beautifully.

And so perhaps this day will start you out
by painting your life
the way you so desire
to be enriched and fulfilled.

And in so doing
you will perhaps fulfill a part of my destiny to be who I am,
a painter of God in my own way.

Godspeed you to the moment,
whatever your moment shall be.

I pray you will be enriched and fulfilled
and that you will be blessed with many gifts
as your life progresses.

Chapter Two
DISCOVERING DESTINY

Dear God,
I pray for strength and inspiration
and guidance over rough waters.
I pray for calm amidst turmoil in my life.
I pray for life to go back to normal for one and all.

Most importantly, I ask that Your healing energy
calms my emotions
so that I may function easily from day to day.
Amen

What is Destiny?

Destiny is what I am here for
and what I have come to accomplish.
It doesn't matter whether I've failed,
or whether I've succeeded.
Perhaps I've come to fail.
Perhaps I've come to succeed.

Either way,
in God's eyes,
I succeed.

In my eyes,
I may have failed miserably.
Yet when I look at my life,
through God's eyes,
I see the huge successes that I have accomplished.

As I discuss 'Painting with God' and Destiny,
Destiny is my first Angel of God.

Destiny is God's Angel
who delivers us safely
from spirit
into this physical reality.

Is Destiny female?
Of course, Destiny is female.
How could she not be female?

She has open arms to embrace you
and what you have come to achieve
in this physical reality.

That is the Angel of Destiny
and we've all been delivered here safely.

And then the Angel of Death
is the one that delivers us back
to where we've come from,
back to Destiny's arms.

Destiny does not come to retrieve us,
rather she sends the Angel of Death –
Her father.

Destiny is also comprised of the people
who come into your life.

I have friends
some of whom have been working with me,
on and off, for 35 years.

And each one has their own unique challenges,
but they're all working on their destiny
as I'm working on mine.
They are discovering more about themselves
and what they desire.

They are open to hearing,
open to listening
and open to Destiny and what she has to offer.

They may be fearful of their own destiny,
fearful of who Destiny is,
fearful of who brought them here
and fearful of who will take them home.
Yet they are searching, desiring, and knowing.

They are loving,
wanting to be loved,
wanting to be discovered
and perhaps today they will discover
a greater part of themselves.

Creativity is a path that one must discover
in their own time,
in their own way.

I have explained to each of my friends
that what they desire of me
is something that I cannot give them
– deliverance.

They each wish to be delivered into a physical reality
where they can manifest.
Only you can manifest in this physical reality -
out of your own choices.

Only you can make things happen
in your reality.

The next angel is the
Angel of the Stars.

The Angel of the Stars
is the angel who gives people souls
and the tools to manifest their gifts.

You can call upon her at any time
to assist you in your career path
and soul seeking journey
of finding your voice.

There is Michael the Archangel
or Michael the Messenger
who you can summon to assist you
in finding your path
and to release the demons that keep you barricaded
and inert.

Michael the Messenger has been with me
helping me constantly in freeing me
from my struggles in this life.

There is also Raphael.
Raphael has been close at my side for some time
healing me,
giving me light and sustenance
and showing me my path.

Raphael is a phenomenal healer.

There is also another angel
who is not generally viewed as an angel.
Many of you know him as Christ,
or the Angel of Christ.

I see Him as an angel,
the Angel of Saints.

Christ has also been assisting me
on my path
for some length of time.

As I navigated the Lake of Lancelot,
another angel appeared on my journey
- the Lady of the Lake.
Many times, I believed the Lady of the Lake
was going to drown me.
She took me over stormy waters and back again,
and delivered me safely on my journey.
I shall call her the Angel of the Lake.

I traveled over troubled waters and faced my fears.
There are many lifetimes where we face
many of the same fears
over and over and over again.

There are so many lifetimes that we go to war
endlessly facing death,
and death faces us and challenges us
and sometimes death succeeds and wins.

Currently in my life, in all our lives,
we are facing potential death with COVID.
We might be fearful that we may succumb to it
with or without God's hands
to save us or to assist us out of it.

More people who are part of my destiny
will come my way.

Of all the angels that I know,
one of the most important
is the Angel of Hope.

Over the past eight months, as I have gone to bed fearful
and woke in the morning fearful,
she has been there by my side sprinkling hope
and seeing me through the darkest periods in my life.

Through all the darkness and nightmares that have
haunted me,
the Angel of Hope has brought me out of it
with thoughts that days will get better,
life will get better and strength will return.
I will be who I have come to be,
a healer, a lover of life,
and to share my gifts with many.

Anyone who desires to heal can heal.
You first must believe.
And, if you believe, you can heal.

If you do not believe,
then a prayer is needed
to find that source within you that lets you believe:

> *Dear God,*
> *As I wake up this morning*
> *and hope has left me,*
> *I fear I am not strong enough*
> *to believe in You,*
> *to believe in Your son Jesus Christ*
> *who has brought many out of difficult times.*

I ask that You deliver me
to Your doorstep of hope and light and understanding.
I pray that You show me
what You are capable of.
I pray that You show me how to believe
that I am worthy of receiving the healings
You send my way.

I pray, Dear God,
You give each one of us
health and happiness.
And if each one of us desires to heal,
then allow us that gift
if we are deserving of it.

I ask Michael the Messenger to lift me up.
And the Angel of Hope to take me in her wings
and fly me to the moon to show me the universe
You have created.
Give me new hope for a new day
and a new opportunity to see
that the universe You have created is at my doorstep
and I am safe with You at all times.
Amen

There are more angels
I would like to mention.
There's an angel very few speak of named
Zachariah, the Angel of Stone.
And often, Zachariah is with those who are stuck in their lives
and unable to move for long periods.

The Angel of Hope
broke me out of the grasp of Zachariah
and set me free.
I have found that dealing with Zachariah
has left me more determined to be stronger
with God's help.

There is Destiny's new husband, Zeus.
Not the Greek God Zeus that you might know
but Zeus the Angel of Emotions and Dreams.
A constant companion of mine in this life.

Zeus is an angel who can make dreams a reality
and has made many of my dreams come true
in the past eight months.

And there is another angel here
I call her Matilda, the Angel of Voices.
Matilda gives each soul their voice
in the physical reality. A voice
that each of you may not yet have found.

If you are working with Matilda, work cautiously,
and be aware you may have a different voice
than what you realize.
We have an expectation of what we want.
What transpires is rarely what we expect.
Be cautious for the voice that you get.
It may not be what you were expecting.

These angels are here to assist you.
I suggest you call upon these angels
and watch what transpires
in a week, two weeks, a month…

As I find my voice
over the next few months,
it will be a new voice.
And as I find my footing, I will be a person
whom I would have never recognized years ago.

As I manifest my new voice in the next few months,
I am destined to embrace the Angel of Success
whom I call the Angel of Diamonds,
Diamond Eyes for short.
Do not call upon her unwittingly
and frivolously thinking that you want success.

Only call upon her
if you believe that she is part of your destiny
and part of your voice from within
for she can also be a master of deception and illusion.

There are so many angels here.
I'm going to talk about the group of angels who heal
called the Dancing Angels.
They're always with us.
If you call upon them,
they will come to you
and assist you with your healing energies and abilities.

The first of these angels is Annabelle, the Angel of Desire.
Annabelle loves all humans and helps us to heal
wanting nothing but joy and happiness
for everyone she works with.
She comes with a great healing light
similar to Raphael and Uriel.
Most angels have healing light.

Annabelle is full of passion.
When you call upon her you may find yourself
becoming a great deal more passionate
about living life to the fullest and desiring things
not wanted previously.

The second one of the Dancing Angels
is Bartholomew, the Angel of Peace.
He has a great deal of knowledge and wisdom
about how to achieve elements of peace and contentment
in your life.
If you call upon Bartholomew,
be prepared to do a lot of hard work spiritually.

The third angel, Nikolai, is the Angel of Fulfillment,
yes, as in old St. Nick who fulfilled many children's dreams.
Nikolai also possesses a strong healing vibration
and works together with Annabelle and Bartholomew.
Why he would be with Annabelle, the Angel of Desire,
and Bartholomew, the Angel of Peace, is simple.
He needs Annabelle and Bartholomew to assist him

in his rituals of dancing to fulfill the requests he has
for healing and bettering health.
In many cases, he makes your dreams come true.

But is the Angel of Fulfillment concerned only with health?
The Angel of Fulfillment at times also works with the
Angel of Destiny
to help people on their quest in life to find purpose
in something meaningful and a reason to be.
So, when you speak of Nikolai, Angel of Fulfillment,
ask yourself what would fulfill you in your quest
to know more about yourself in your life.

As one ages and grows in wisdom
and realizes health as their greatest asset,
health can often make one feel fulfilled,
joyful and thankful for what they have.

These Dancing Angels also dance.
Do not be surprised if at times
you find yourself light on your feet.
Why dance?
Well, dancing is like singing.
It can heal and soothe the pain of life's troubled waters.
I leave you with the Dancing Angels
who come as a group
to heal those in need of physical, emotional, spiritual
and mental healing.

Take the time to become aware of angels.
Angels are as real as God is real.
Take away the air you breathe,
you take away God.

Take away God, you die.
So, breathe deeply
and when you breathe deeply and meditate,
know that you are breathing with God
and living with God.

I am just learning to live with God.

Many blessings to all of you
who have come to share in the writing
and making of this wonderful
fascinating journey called
'Painting with God'.

Chapter Three
SOUL MATES - WHAT IS LOVE?

My Prayer is:

Dear God,
If dreams come true
I'd be with You.
Amen

I want to talk about the years of my youth
spent seeking a soulmate.

We all desire love in one form or another
and, like many, I looked and looked
and searched and searched for many years
for a soulmate.
Someone who would compliment me
in EVERYTHING I did.

Now, in my later years,
I look at it much more differently.
Not from someone who is young and naïve or inexperienced,
but more from someone who has grown through the hardships
of relationships not working nor manifesting in a way
I had dreamed they would.

Now I see relationships are very much about finding someone
who is kind, compassionate and empathetic.

If any of you have found that,
then you are truly fortunate.

And if you are still seeking and searching,
then look in the mirror
and ask yourself:
Am I kind?
Am I giving?
Am I empathetic?
Am I compassionate?

Have I learned my lessons?

If the answer is 'no'
to any of those questions,
then it is time for you to become that person.
That person that you want in your life.

Find it in your heart to be kind,
forgiving,
compassionate,
and empathetic.
Those are very tall orders to fill
and with each one you adopt comes much wisdom.

My prayer is:

Dear God,
I ask to more clearly understand what I am looking for in my ideal relationship.
Is it love that I seek? Is it
Companionship?
Someone to share time with?
Someone to have a friendship with?
Or perhaps, a love relationship?

God, I ask for Your guidance
today and always
as I venture out into the world
in search of more meaning to my life
and in search of a greater understanding of You
and a greater understanding of myself.

We all hope and dream of love
but that is not necessarily what we really desire.

I pray today God,
that You take my hand and show me this person
whose core being resonates with my core being.
One individual to accompany me along my journey in this life.

Show me how to express myself creatively
by any means
that will assist me to grow in Your loving light.
Amen

Chapter Four
WHAT LIES AHEAD – TAROT

My prayer is a simple one.

Dear God,
As I struggle with my emotions constantly challenging me
through stress, depression and fears of COVID entering my body,
I ask You to balance and heal my emotions
with Your limitless energy, love and light.

I pray for those around me who also struggle.
With new hope and support,
may they too be lifted up by Your loving hands
and given another chance
to heal emotionally and physically.

I pray that through Your love, forgiveness, and compassion
You show me the way out of the dark and into the light.

I thank You for Your endless healings
that lift me and give me hope
and for the friends and loved ones
who constantly watch out over me.
Amen

This may seem like a simple task
to write something of this nature,
to find the right words, thoughts,
expressions and the ideas to put down on paper.

The thoughts over the weeks, months and years
have rumbled through my mind

along with the insight and knowledge that God and my
guides have shown me over time,
all must be dissected, drawn out, and given expression.

Let's imagine a tarot deck with angels.
And let's suppose
we have Michael, the Archangel,
show up in your tarot reading.

Michael would symbolize
strength and protection ahead
in all the things you are about to undertake.

The Lady of the Lake
indicates troubled waters ahead, emotionally,
or even rough waters,
where you may find yourself
losing your footing and balance.
It is the time to be incredibly cautionary
when it comes to your personal world,
relationships and business.

Raphael being the healer
symbolizes issues around health
that need your attention and focus,
and need to be addressed.
Or perhaps you are
already working on your health.

As I do a virtual reading for myself,
I see both the Angel of Stars
and the Angel of Diamond Eyes,
although the Angel of Stars has a more prominent presence.

And this is certainly something hugely significant
for she is one who expresses outward notoriety and success.

Another angel that comes to mind
is Destiny,
the Angel of Destiny.

Why Destiny?
Well, she symbolizes success.
I also see her with the Angel of Hope.
Currently, in my life, I'm moving towards greater health and greater expression of myself.
Where opportunities are abounding with my art I am painting, my work in music in creating another album and my work in writing this book.
A tarot deck with angels would show me that these things are coming to pass.
I see ahead there will be public interest in much of what I am doing.

As I write, I feel very strongly
that after all my struggles
my emotions are now changing.

They're becoming much more solidified
and my health is growing more balanced and stronger.
I feel healthier and stronger.
I see good things ahead.

As I write this,
I pray that everything is working itself out.

Chapter Five
HEALING

My prayer for healing is this:

Dear God,
In all Your divine energy,
light and love,
I pray You show me
what I need to know about healing.

How can I be an instrument of Your healing?
How can I help others to heal?
How can I allow myself to heal from my past,
from my present moments of difficulties
and from the physical and emotional challenges?

I pray You help me to know
how to surrender to the higher power of Your light
so that I may heal emotionally, physically and mentally.

I pray You release me
from the burdens that I carry
each and every day.

I pray You also help those
who are close to and around me
and that they too be able to release
their burdens, pain and struggles
they carry each day.

I pray for all those in the world
who struggle with mental distress and anxiety.

I pray for myself with my own challenges,
struggles and anxiety.

I pray You lift me up and help me
to release these struggles and
to see and believe in Your light and Your love,
Your forgiveness and compassion,
and Your understanding and acceptance.

I pray this evening
You embrace me
and so many others who are reaching out
for Your love and assistance with healing energy.

I pray You show me
how to tap the divine energy within me within my soul
and help me to ignite it in healing myself
and in healing others
who may be seeking me out for higher knowledge,
understanding, learning and healing.

Allow me to be a beacon
of Your love and light
in whatever way that I can.
Help me to resist the temptation
of being angry and resentful.

Help me to see
that there is so much to be grateful for.
Help me to see
that anger does nothing but cause distress,
pain and struggle for me and those around me.

Help me to heal through forgiveness and
other means that You see best for me.

I pray You show me the way
through these struggles.
Amen

I would like to discuss further
your abilities to heal.
You have within you the capability to heal.
Whether you wish to heal yourself or
those close to you or
those that you love,
all is possible if you believe.

The true secret to healing is
in believing that God ignites the eternal flame
to heal yourself and those that you love and care about.

If you see yourself as a healer,
then be an instrument of God's love and light.
Let that light flow through you.
As it flows through you
to heal those around you,
believe that they're being healed.
What is most important is that you believe
you can heal.
Ask God for strength to believe,
to know beyond a shadow of a doubt,
you are capable of being exceptional at abilities
you don't even know you possess.

Healing is something
most individuals live their entire life never knowing
they can have such a phenomenal gift.
Yet, it's important to recognize
that healing physically, mentally, emotionally or spiritually,
comes in different ways.

There are so many ways to heal.
You can heal through prayer.
You can heal through meditation.
You can heal through believing.
You can heal through picturing yourself full of light,
or filling others with light
and allowing the guides and the
angels from above to assist.

As you reach out to help others heal
and to heal yourself,
here's a suggested prayer to begin with:

God is with me wherever I go.
I am an instrument of His love,
His light, His nourishment.
I believe that God can heal through me with
God's guidance, with God's love,
with God's acceptance and with God's understanding.

Here and now I choose to surrender to God's Higher
Power that will allow me the opportunity to be that
light that
possesses healing energy.

And with this light that passes through me,
I choose to utilize it to heal others
and to heal myself.
Amen

Miracles exist and you are capable with those miracles
to heal yourself or others that you care about and love.
And the stronger you believe, the more capable you will be.

In all that I choose in my life as I move forward,
I choose God to release me
from the struggles of every day anxiety.
I choose God to give me a voice, a prayer, and an answer
to solve struggles and problems
that are causing me such great anxiety.

With all these prayers,
I hope and pray that as you read this
you will see that there is not one perfect way
to God's healing energy.

I leave you with this simple thought.
God has all the answers to all your problems.

If you trust and believe,
then God will bring you those answers quickly and easily.

Dear God,
I pray for strength and inspiration
and guidance over rough waters.
I pray for calm amidst turmoil in my life.
I pray for life to go back to normal for one and all.

Most importantly I ask that Your healing energy
calms my emotions
so that I may function easily from day to day.
Amen

Chapter Six
SURRENDERING TO LOVE

This is my prayer:

> *Dear God,*
> *Teach me how to love,*
> *how to let love in*
> *and how to surrender to love.*
> *Amen*

As I look back over the years,
I found that love has been kind to me,
relationships have been good to me
and I have been fortunate.

Did I ever realize in my twenties, thirties, forties or even fifties
how fortunate I was
with all the prospects of relationships
and those who I was interested in romantically, or otherwise?
Did I see my good fortune at my doorstep?

No, unfortunately I did not see how fortunate I was.
There was so much of love
and desiring of love that I took for granted.

I never acknowledged my good fortune.
I never realized that God had blessed me
with so many assets and attributes
I just took for granted.

And now looking back in hindsight,
sadly, there is so much regret
because I see that I wasted so much time not seeing,
not taking inventory, not appreciating, not acknowledging
and not accepting that God had given me
numerous opportunities
and had blessed me beyond belief.

For years I had just assumed that love had passed me by
and would never come my way.
Now as I look back, I realize that I chose to not see.
I chose to not look.
I chose to not understand
that I was not ugly or unfortunate or unwanted.

That was how I chose to see myself
because I felt it was a fit for me.
That is what I chose to believe
but the truth and the reality were far from that.
Now, I chuckle to myself realizing that my eyes were
so closed.
Life was so good in so many ways
and I did not see it.

And so, with my prayer to God
I wish for you to see that opportunity is at your door for
the taking
if you so desire to see it,
if you so desire to truly want it.

Open your eyes.
Open your heart.
Open your life to love
and do not expect love to come visit you in any
particular way.
Love owes you nothing.
God owes you nothing.
No male or female owes you anything.
If someone comes to your door,
feel blessed and fortunate that they have.
Accept that God smiles upon you.

God paints the kaleidoscope of love
that we so often ignore.

Perhaps we can expand our horizons,
express more about ourselves,
learn that God once again has arrived at our door
to tell us:
"Hey kids you're never too old to love.

You're never too old to learn.
You're never too old to try.
You're never too old to smile."
Love is not about someone looking at you
and seeing nothing but beauty.
Love is about an opportunity
that God gives you without a price tag.
Love is all around you.

When you buy cut flowers at the store,
you buy them because they will express an emotion
or a feeling that you have.
Yet flowers are often a very strong element of love
that we give ourselves.

So, the next time you buy flowers love them.
Love that they are an expression of yourself,
another aspect of yourself that God is showing you
how to paint a beautiful painting of your life.

Take that opportunity to broaden it,
to add colour to it,
to see that life is to be cherished,
not taken for granted.

Love is not something you can possess or own.
It is not something that someone needs to give you or
owes you.
If someone decides to be with you,
they are not your prisoner nor are you theirs.

Love is about sharing
and taking time to explore the many horizons
that come from day to day.
Nurture those horizons,
explore them,
grow with them
and see the vastness of opportunity.

The past number of months I have prayed often
and asked God to show me my path,
my way, my future.

I've asked to be led out of the darkness
and to see more clearly what there is to be explored.
Each day I see more and each day I learn more.

Some days are happier than others.
I'm still growing and learning
and hoping and praying that I will get back
and reacquaint with the person
I once knew.

Perhaps you will become acquainted with your youthful side.
Explore, embrace, develop, and play with your youthful side.

Be at peace with what you believe you should be, or should have been.
Release it and surrender to it.

And that is what we need to do in love.

We need to surrender to that which we cannot control.
Love cannot be caged.
Love is not there for our bidding.
Love is not there to do
as we demand of it.
We are there to surrender to it.
And if we do not surrender to it, then
it will not be there
and we miss the boat.

I pray God soon releases me from the struggles
I've had in recent months
so I may get on with my life
that God presents and unfolds before me.

I wish to share with you those avenues
presented to me and given freely by God,
not with a price tag and not with a 'have to'
but simply for me to grow, to learn, to see,
to understand and to accept.

Love requires acceptance.
I must accept a part of myself that I cannot change.

I need to accept the weak and frail side of myself
that cannot dominate love nor possess love
but can only cherish it.
I hope and pray that it stays until my time has come
to return from where I came - in spirit.

Recently, I have been receiving inspiration
to create another album of music
and to write lyrics for six, seven or eight more songs
and to once again express myself through my voice.

I anticipate that my heart will be full
and that God will stand behind or beside me and help
me to sing,
help me to express, to grow and to understand.
God is helping me to paint
this beautiful painting of my life,
the expressive side I want to believe is there
as much as I think it is there.

Take the time to explore those sides of yourself
that you do not believe you can manifest.
Take a risk and go out and do things
that you don't think you can do.
Be you, a great version of you.
Be strong.

Stand fast and go
and know beyond a shadow of a doubt
that God wants you to be the best you want to be.
All those desires within you
are to be expressed,
not to be denied or hidden.

Let yourself express love. Let yourself be love.
And yet, let yourself surrender
to that which you cannot own or possess.

Do not be afraid to succumb to love's powers and strength
over your own.
Let it be that which shows you the value in life
that there are so many things

that we do not understand about God.
That God is an expression of love
and yet God goes even beyond love.

There are no words that can describe what God is.
God is a kaleidoscope of love to me,
a kaleidoscope of expression and languages,
many of which I may never understand or know
but I have the opportunity to try.

I want to be something
that I do not believe that I can be
- an infinite energy of God's love.

So tomorrow when I wake up,
I want to be something more than I am today.
I want to be a greater expression of God.
I want to live.
I want to love.
I want to learn.
I want to know.

And with all of what I say,
I hope you see the opportunity to paint your life with God
in brilliant colours and expressions
being the best you can be.

Go beyond what you think you are.
Become somebody you do not think you are.
Express something great about yourself.
Challenge yourself to be something
more than what you are now.

With that, you can only win
and be successful in your life.

With your life fulfilled beyond your wildest dreams,
I pray to God we all get to know even just a small aspect
of who God is.

Chapter Seven
DISCOVER WHO YOU ARE

I would like to elaborate a bit more
about those entities in the spirit world
that are there to assist you.

Beginning with Archangel Destiny,
Archangel Destiny is there to assist you with direction,
and helping you find your way when you are lost.

If you feel like you've lost your path,
not making progress in your career,
or in your personal life,
or you may be striving to create your own business,
Archangel Destiny is there to get you back on track.
There are so many avenues that she can assist you with.

Michael the Messenger, Archangel Michael is God's warrior and
is also one to bring you messages from God.
In your prayers, if you ask Michael directly for his insight and assistance,
you may receive a direct message from the Divine Light called God,
and you will know it's from God.
There is a certain sense and feeling
that comes with messages from God.

Michael traveled often with Christ on His path
and assisted Him in all things,
especially in always protecting Him and keeping Him safe.

Michael the Archangel is also an Angel of Safety.
If you are frightened or fearful, he can assist you.
He comes with a sense of safety and a feeling of protection.

If you wish to protect your loved ones,
ask Michael to be around them
and to alert you if there is a problem.
Stay connected with him on an ongoing basis
and relax into the feeling of protection.

There are so many archangels I have come to know
and as the days progress and I continue to write,
I will share with you these archangels' attributes.

I'm aware you may not believe in miracles.
Once you experience a miracle, there is no doubt.

If a miracle is what you are looking to experience,
Christ is the one to turn to.
Who other could assist you with miracles in your life than
Jesus Christ?
Who did miracles for the multitudes?
Who brought Lazarus back from the dead?
Christ healed those with leprosy and did other
phenomenal miracles.

These miracles are possible if one believes.
It is obvious that Jesus came with the ability
to not only believe, but to manifest
and so, for each of you as you develop your ability to believe,
so will your gifts greatly increase with time.

Over the years my intuitive abilities have become
second nature.
My abilities to heal are still growing.
I am more here to assist you, to recognize
that you too can heal yourself and those around you
if you are willing to access those gifts within you.

And through prayer and acknowledgement
and acceptance and surrender,
these gifts will come to pass over time.

You may be already naturally gifted with these gifts.
You may be a natural healer,
but even a natural healer needs to hone their abilities
and skills.
Begin to nurture your abilities
and watch them grow.

Chapter Eight
INSPIRATION

I often get asked what inspires me to paint
and how do I create such beautiful work?

My desire to be closer to God inspires me to paint.

When I paint, I have a sense of God being with me
that drives me to do more and more amazing works.

Which are the best paintings?

I can never tell because I start with a blank canvas
and over weeks or even years it may develop into
something spectacular.
Or literally it may simply be days
where my intuition shows me something mesmerizing.

With each painting I do comes a sense of
absolute satisfaction
when complete.
It's not about selling my art that drives me forward.
It's that sense of knowing God, being with God,
and feeling and growing with God daily.

I have painted in winter,
spring, summer and fall.
Is there a season that I favour over others to paint?
No, each season is different.
Each day is different.
I may not paint for months as winter comes along
and then one day I might take a room in the house and
I start to paint.
As always, there is something spectacular or
an all-encompassing energy that fulfills me
as I finish another day of painting.

It is up to you to decide what you want to create with God.
What do you want to manifest?
What is something that you enjoy doing?
Find it, nurture it, and let God grow with you.

It might be writing poetry.
It might be bird watching.
It might be growing and caring for a garden.
There are so many different options to get closer to God.
So many that we take for granted every day.

Sometimes when I lay in bed at night, I pray.
With those prayers, I find myself closer to God, Who speaks the language of silence.
As I listen closely to what God has to say,
inspiration comes from that silence.

If you could ask God one thing,
knowing that God would reply,
what would you ask?

Reconnect spiritually with that God within you.

Over time many of us have lost that connection and strength.
Our search is something we often don't manage to realize in life.
Outwardly we might look for money, status,
power, material possessions,
but what is it that we truly seek?

We're really looking to reconnect with God.
To find that place in the universe that is ours,
that is meaningful,
something that is tangible.

Eventually, we all must pass into spirit.
We go back to where we came from
- the God source, the God energy.

I have had my share of encounters to see and to know God
in ways that I had never expected,
and they have fulfilled me in so many ways.

Start a conversation with your God.
Speak with your God.
Speak with the voice within you,
or you may hear it as a voice outside of yourself.

Speak and find and reconnect with a part of you
that you may not know or have lost.

As you reconnect, discover that greater purpose in your life.
A purpose that brings you a great deal more satisfaction
than any material gains or position of status
or whatever it is you may be seeking outwardly in the world.

That is left to be seen, only by you.
You are the only one that can make that happen.
The choice is always yours.

Chapter Nine
GOD CAME TO ME

Four or five years back,
over the course of six months,
God came to me several times
in my dreams.
One of those times, He appeared as a burning bush
and at another He appeared in the form of a tree.

For months on end
I felt happier than ever in my life
and learned that happiness existed.
I never had the experience
of being happy.

I once believed happiness was just a state of mind
or that we want to believe ourselves to be happy.
Never before that time had I experienced being happy,
and for the first time in my life
I could truly and honestly say
I was happy.

The idea of writing this book came
to me over the period of a few months.
There was nothing I wanted more
than to write a book about painting with God
because I did and I do.
I paint with God.

From the time I started painting nine or ten years ago,
I discovered whenever I finished a painting that I liked
I was moved.
God was with me,
not painting for me necessarily,
but moving within me
and I was in awe.

I was always overwhelmed with the beauty of the colours and
the feeling I would be left with.
Sometimes the feeling would be exquisite,

and I might think,
"Oh, this painting is done".

A few days later, I'd look back and think
"no, it's not done yet".
Weeks and months would pass
or even a year or two would pass
and I would finally finish the painting.
When I finished it, it would seem brilliant to me.
It always ended up being something
that was beautiful to my eyes.

I always felt God in my presence
when completing a painting.
I felt God each time I painted.

So, when the title 'Painting with God' came to me,
there was nothing to think about.
This was the right title for this book
because God has inspired me
so often throughout my life
and I am grateful for it.

Now, as I work through personal difficulties and my aging,
God still inspires me constantly.

In the past, I worked at developing my intuition
for 20 or so years
before retiring from the public eye
as a spiritual teacher and advisor.
During that time,
I became closer to my guides and teachers in spirit.
As I moved forward, I came to know more of God and
I still find myself firmly rooted in God.

Over the past 30 years,
my personal difficulties and challenges along the way
have, from time to time, made me question God
or have made me question why I have come
and why I have put myself through
such difficulties in this life.

As I look around and see others
in much worse circumstances than I am dealing with,
I realize how fortunate I am
and what I have been given.

I work at trying to be thankful,
and it is work.
It's not something that is simple,
nor something that is easy.

In this day and age
where many diseases like cancer
are running rampant,
and so many people are sick,
I think to myself
if only we remembered to give thanks
and realized that God is a forgiving God.
Our God is a loving God.
Our God, my God, understands and sees what I do not see.
I do not see my weaknesses and my faults.

And if my God sees them and still accepts me
and loves me for who I am,
then disease is not a sin.
It is not a punishment.
It is a learning process for us to grow with
and grow we do.

During this period of my life,
I've asked myself what it is
that I really want for the remaining years of my life
whether it be 5, 10 or 20.

I can't see it.
But what do I want for those remaining years?

The answer came back as a resounding
"I do not know".
Then I think back
to when I was 29, 39 or 49,
did I know then what I wanted?
Even though I thought I did,

I didn't because I was young and naive.
And, now I'm older and naive.

What pushes me forward?
Again, I don't know
what pushes me forward.

Dear Jesus,
do any of us know what pushes us forward?

And even as I speak these words,
I foresee writing a series of books,
one titled 'Dear Jesus'.
I often turn to Christ for answers
for faith, for healing
and to ease the burdens on my shoulders.
Jesus does know and gives
so much more than I will ever know or see.

Now you may never paint with God,
but maybe you will sing with God
or talk with God.
Some night when you are sleeping
God may come to you and speak to you
and what a joyous occasion it would be.

Begin to develop a repertoire
or an ongoing conversation with God during the day,
or at night before turning into sleep.
Talk to God, find God, reveal God, believe in God.

Believe in your God
and then discover what that will do for you.

What has it done for me?
It's allowed me a reason to live
and a reason to enjoy life to the fullest.

Take inventory of all the things
you have to be thankful for.
Sooner or later, as you age,
these things will slowly but surely dissolve.

Enjoy the things of youth
and as you age
enjoy what wisdom brings.

Enjoy what God is teaching you with age.
Recognize that wisdom is priceless.
Peace and quiet and silence are priceless.
Speak to your God within you.
Listen to the silence
and you will hear God.

Someday when the wind is blowing,
take a deep breath,
put your back to the wind
and say to yourself:

> *"God is the wind,*
> *God is the air I breathe",*

and take God in,
embrace God
and recognize God is all around you.
God is all around each of us.
Each and every person in your life
is a part of God.

Chapter Ten
ONE SOUL

We have all come as one soul. How ironic is that?
We are all one soul
and we are connected by a thin thread.
We may not even recognize
that we are all a part of the same puzzle.
We all fit together in the bigger scheme of things
though we might not see it.

Recognize that your brother or your sister
or your neighbour or your friends,
regardless of the colour of their skin,
or the language they speak,
are a part of you.
They are a part of the greater picture.

When you realize that everyone is a part of you
then, and only then,
can you see God and the bigger picture.

In my life, I've experienced the loves,
the pain of losing someone you love,
the heartache of sickness and death,
and of abandonment and of betrayal.
These were all significant lessons in my life.
Without betrayal and without abandonment,
what would I have learned?
Where would I be if I did not learn what to value?

So, when people value you,
love you or care about you,
those are the ones to embrace.
Those are the ones to pour your love into.
Those are the ones to recognize as your true friends
and the ones of incredible value.

The ones who value you,
value everything about you.
If you ever have the good fortune of a friend saying to you,

"I so love being with you",
"I so enjoy my time with you",
you don't have to respond immediately.
Those are the individuals
you never want to lose.

The ones you want to keep
are the ones who have their eyes open
and their tongues moving.
These lessons might seem to be incredibly difficult and painful
yet, over time, they too shall all pass.

We move on to the next wave,
the next life
and the next major lesson that we have come to learn.

Throughout my life I've asked myself time and time again
"what have I come to learn?".
It's simple.
I've come to learn that I am foolish.
For only being foolish as I have been
could I possibly not see
the wondrous amazing gifts
I have been given in this life.

And they were and are amazing gifts.

I have been able to see my past lives.
I've been able to see my future.
I've been able to see my friends
and who they are.
I have been able to tap into and understand life
in ways that others have not.
I can feel things more deeply than many can.

Those are all gifts.
They are gifts that help me to see
that God is around me
and is with me all the time.
My gifts have shown me over time
just how precious all of us are.

So, when you decide to paint with God,
paint something in your mind or in your soul
that is exquisite.
Sit down and write a letter to God
and tell God how you feel
and how exquisite you believe God is.

God is simply a mirror of ourselves.

If you see beauty,
then you are seeing God as that reflection of you.
Take your time to look more deeply.
Take your time to see.
Take your time to paint.
It is never too late to find God.
It is never too late to find yourself.
It is never too late to start something creative
that inspires you.
Whether it is painting or writing or singing,
it doesn't matter what it is,
inspire yourself
to become something exceptional to you,
not to anyone else.
Do it simply for you.

In this life, I have had the good fortune
to access the drive to persist and achieve things
that in my youth I never dreamed I would achieve.

I have had amazing and wonderful friends.
I have loved, lost and been my own best friend
and my own worst enemy.
Through it all I have cared deeply and profoundly for others
and I have felt the losses
as I have come through each step,
whether with them in hand or not.

I have learned that I can deceive and fool myself.
At times I have not seen the value in others.
Often it was much later that I saw the value
in people who meant a great deal to me.

Everything takes time.
I have often thought I was smart
and paid the price for thinking I was,
only to realize
I did not have the answers
nor did I look, listen or pay attention.

Look, Listen, and watch,
and life reveals itself.
It's really that simple.
Life reveals itself.

It is so much easier
when you trust your heart and your soul.
If you just listen to silence, you may hear the guides
and the souls that gather around you
to assist you
as you go through this physical vibration.

You have a guardian angel.
Everyone has one.

Everyone has a guardian angel,
and you can pick an archangel if you so choose.
Ask any angels to be with you.
You can ask Christ to walk with you.
You can ask God to walk with you.

Can you ask anyone in spirit to walk with you?
Do they have choice
as to whether they will walk with you?
Everyone has choice.
When you ask for help from the spirit world,
they see it is as a golden opportunity.

What is spirit's mission in the realm of spirit?
What is the purpose of the angels,
archangels and souls on that side
who watch out over souls on this side?
Their purpose is to gain wisdom,
to learn and to grow with the person
navigating in this physical reality.

If I could explain in simple terms
what it's been like painting with God,
I could not possibly put a price tag on my
conversations with God
or speaking with God.

The voice of God - you do not forget.
It resonates in the very core of who you are,
a voice that you recognize as a Father of all.
A voice that can leave you speechless
or render you speechless or paralyzed
simply because there is such awe and depth to that voice.

Is it possible that God can heal and transform you
without the use of medication and physical tools?
Yes, God heals.
Do I believe deeply enough
for God to heal me?
I can only wait and see
and test myself to see if
I am worthy of a healing.

Am I worthy of God's miracles?
What makes any of us worthy?
What are you willing to sacrifice for others in
your willingness to give?
How willing are you to believe
and what makes you worthy is how
much you are willing to give.

We have been given the world by God
and many of us don't even thank God for that world
or that opportunity.
To believe and to give and accept
and to acknowledge what we have been given
and to give to others is what makes us worthy.

Do I look to be materially wealthy before I die?
Money will never make me happy,
no more than a big empty house will make me happy.
Money to me is just a big, empty house.

I want my house to be full and rich
with people who I care about.
Open your house to charity.
Open your life to charity.
Open your life to giving.
Open your life to show yourself
that others do not have what you have.
Open your eyes and see
that there are others out there
who need your help,
who do not have the gifts
that you have been given.
And so, it is up to you to give to others
and to sacrifice.

Giving isn't just handing out to get a receipt.
Giving is when something inside of you hurts
and you do not want to give that up,
and only that is giving.
If it does not hurt, you are not giving.
You must give from a place
where you want to keep that material possession
you are giving.
The more you learn to let it go,
the wiser you become.

I have sought to give as much as possible.
I've known that giving makes me feel better
and it has never proven me wrong.
Right now, I am looking to heal emotionally and
somewhat physically.
I am asking God to show me the path
and give me the ability to recognize
how I can heal myself.

I'm hoping this book will guide you along the path
to heal yourself and find it within yourself
to forgive yourself for what you believed.
You might think that you've done something wrong,
or you haven't done something right.

I hope it is clear in illustrating to you
how God can help you to see.
God can bring you the opportunity to grow.
God can bring you the opportunity to love
but above all God can bring you the opportunity to heal.
And why I am here
and why Destiny has brought me here
with her loving arms
is so I can heal my soul
and get back to my God.

This is my prayer to you:

Dear Jesus,
I pray You will walk with me
and take me home with You as You go.
Amen

So perhaps, you too, can find Jesus
and walk with Jesus or Mother Mary
or whoever you choose
and that they help you to find your way home
to the heart and soul and core of you
that is God.
There is no greater wish I could have for you.
If and when you discover God,
pray that God, your God, brings you home safely
and that your God heals you
with every step along your path home.
For we have all come to be healed.
We are all seeking healing.
We are all seeking to be one with God.
The greater picture that we are all linked as one.

I pray my friends also find their path home safely.
They are here also to help me to heal.
That is a phenomenal and an exceptional opportunity
to heal physically and emotionally.
To know that beyond a shadow of a doubt
that God is with me, healing me.
What an exceptional opportunity I have been given.

And as I heal,
I pray God will carry me home.

As you go through this book, page by page,
I do hope and pray I am inspiring each of you to be the child of God
that you so desire to be and discover
and to recognize that as a child of God,
you deserve to be here.
You deserve to find your way home.
You deserve love.
You deserve joy.
And perhaps above all, you deserve to be happy.

When you pray,
know the more you discover your God,
the more you will come to understand
what I have understood about happiness
that it truly does exist.
I leave you with my love, light
and understanding of my insight with spirit.
I wish all of you the best on your journey.

Chapter Eleven
ARCHANGEL MOTHER EARTH

Another archangel I have come to know as Elizabeth
who is not mentioned in the Bible,
is Archangel Mother Earth.
She is here to look after our planet
and its physical keeping.

Elizabeth has been around since the beginning of time
as an earthly angel
and one who has two realities,
one in spirit and one on the physical plane.

Elizabeth is also known as Mother Nature.
I refer to her as Mother Earth.

What can you pray to Elizabeth for?

You can ask for earthly appreciation,
acknowledgment, acceptance
and understanding of your physical reality
and of all that surrounds you.

You can pray for physical beauty in your environment,
such as your home, your workplace
and anywhere you spend a good deal of time.

Elizabeth will assist you
in creating an atmosphere that is enjoyable or beautiful.

Dear Mother Earth,
I thank You for all the beauty that surrounds me,
for the sun, the earth, the sky,
the stars, the moon and the planets above in the universe.

I pray You reveal to me
all the beauty that surrounds me daily
and that my eyes are open to greater acceptance.

Help me to grow my love for all of nature,
the trees, the plants and the animals.

Help me to see the beauty You created
that You take care of and take pride in
so that I may take pride and joy in all of it as well
for it all is a part of me.

The earth is my backyard and I pray
You show me how to better appreciate what I have
been given and how to maintain and improve my world
each day.

How can I improve my physical environment at work?
How can I improve my home and my surroundings
each day?

I pray You show me avenues
to creating greater beauty in the world around me.

Elizabeth, I pray You guide me
and show me all that is true.
Amen

Maybe the next prayer is to yourself:

Please help me to improve my environment every day,
the world I work in and the home I live in.
Help me to keep beauty and peace around me.
Help me to create the atmosphere that puts me at
ease.

If you choose, the prayer can be to God.

These are things that do not limit you.
These archangels have strength.
They have great beauty at their disposal
and it is something that is worthy of us to recognize.

Just like you might pray to canonized saints,
angels too can help you through
to a more gratifying journey in this physical world.

Chapter Twelve
HEALING CONTINUES

I would like to talk about healing.
What does it mean to heal?
I experience healing as energy. It's a vibration.
An energy can change your physical body
and it can help your body be stronger.
Energy, therefore, can heal you of disease, sickness,
colds or a flu.

When you come down with a flu,
you might notice towards the end
you begin to feel stronger and more energetic.

You start getting back to normal,
eating again and feeling better.

If you have a healing or know how to create a healing energy,
it is possible for energy to heal you
so that you get over your cold or flu quicker.

If you can find a healer
or if you know how to change your own vibration,
know of enough prayers,
or in some cases chant,
these things can also help in healing.
When you change your vibration through energy, which I call
healing energy, you can feel better more quickly.

The Bible tells us that Christ healed individuals with leprosy
as well as healed many more people who had other diseases.
He even raised Lazarus from the dead.
How did He do that?

Well, let's suppose it was energy, phenomenal energy,
capable to change one's physical vibration.
If Christ was able to heal individuals physically
when He was alive,
those miracles are still possible today in one form or another.
We need to unlock the key to be able to learn how to

heal people from deadly disease and sickness.
How is that possible?

When one meditates, one slows down their breathing
and their consciousness slips into their subconscious
which then gives one more clarity.
Your vibration is different.

Your breathing changes your physical reality
for a short period of time while meditating
and when you return to the normal awake state,
you're apt to feel better afterwards.

Why do you feel better?

When you link to your subconscious mind,
you link with a healing energy that you possess inwardly.
That connection allows us the ability to heal ourselves.
Your subconscious mind has healing powers
that most of us are not even aware of.

How do we access those powers that are in the subconscious?
How do we access that healing energy?

Over the years of working with spirit
and working with my knowledge of God,
I have come to know there are many things
we do not understand,
one of them being the power of God
that is within us and that supposedly lies within our soul.

We cannot see our souls, or can we?
Our soul is the energy we have been created from.
To link in with it links us with many lifetimes.
We link with the great power that lies within our soul.
When we go to the subconscious, through meditation,
we link in with our soul. When we link in with our soul,
we link in with all the lifetimes in which we have
previously existed, and therein lies the secrets to life.

The secret or secrets to life lie within us.
The healing powers to heal ourselves

also live within our subconscious.
How do you access this great divine power within you?

Start through prayer.

Recognize that God is all powerful
and that God can help us access our healing power
if we deserve and believe it is possible.

One has to want to link with that ability to heal.
One has to want to link with a deeper part of yourself,
the God energy that resides within you.
There is a God energy that resides outwardly that is a
God energy, but there is an energy that resides within us that
is also a part of God.

To put it simply, this all goes back to God.
God is the Creator of all things.
We access all of this through a higher power that I call God.
Within each of you is a God energy
and let's suppose we call this God energy the Kundalini.
When you access your Kundalini,
then and only then, can you know the true power of healing.

When you link with your Kundalini, be aware it is
incredibly powerful
and can stir your emotions creating physical stress by
unlocking that divine secret.
Why would it cause great stress to unlock that secret?
Well, because it is the unknown and we all fear the unknown.
We fear what we do not know or understand, and in our world,
and in our society, we do not believe or understand the
subconscious.

We have not spent a great deal of time studying it or
accessing its great potential,
and there is a phenomenal amount of potential in
the subconscious.
To heal, you must first access the subconscious
power and potential.
As you access it, and your Kundalini,
then you can heal yourself and those around you.

When you go to church, or a temple of prayer,
you can access an energy or power
you do not believe is within you.
Why can you do this at a temple or at a church and
not at home?
Well, because you not only have your energy,
but many other people's energy around you who are
also praying.
You, therefore, have more energy to access,
more strength, more power within you.

Many people praying together have great strength and power.
When you do access your ability to heal
you will feel like there is nothing that you cannot do
or accomplish.
My suggestion to each of you, who are reading this,
is if you want to develop your healing abilities you must
first pray,
then you must learn to, on some level, meditate.
Through that meditation and that silence,
you can access your God,
the God that is within you.

Now is meditation the only way of accessing the God
within you?
No. Prayer is an avenue to access it.
Years of prayer, years of even doing yoga
can take you physically into yourself into a meditative state
that will help you to access your subconscious.
The power is within you.

Psychics or mediums often throughout their lifetime,
as they delve deeper and deeper into studying the occult,
find they have healing powers or knowledge of
healing powers.
They discover over time they have a lot of access
to knowledge and insights into life that others do not have.
How do they have this?
Well, they have this through accessing their subconscious
and using their intuition to tune in with other people.
This is a gift.

It's an ability that's been given at birth.
It may be passed down through the family
because families carry such gifts and abilities.

The psychic can or does know on a certain level
that there is a God that does exist.
There is knowledge of God.
There is knowledge of information
that typically they're not used to having
or that the average person does not yet have access to.
The psychic or the medium has access to this unknown knowledge.
Why?
Well, because they are gifted with access to
the subconscious.
Can anyone access this knowledge?
Over time, yes, anyone can if they are working towards it.
If they're doing prayer and if they are studying it,
then, yes, why shouldn't they or why couldn't they?
It is open to anyone if one so desires to learn.
Yet, if you have no knowledge of the occult,
spirituality, knowing past lives
or healing or things of that nature,
are you really going to want to try to access that
through a medium or a psychic if you know nothing about it?
You may not because it may frighten you
since it is again the unknown.

Each and every individual has so much potential
that they are unaware of.
Phenomenal potential to be stronger, to be healthier,
to have more insight, to see the future,
to see the past and
to see deeper into the present moment of all three together, past, present and future.
Supposedly, Father, Son and the Holy Ghost depending on how you desire to look at it.

If you look at angels and archangels,
who are you praying to?
Who are you accessing when you pray to them,
or when you talk to them,
while you're speaking to souls in spirit?
Well, where is spirit?
Apparently, that is where people reside who are dead.
Each of you are living in the home for the living
in the physical reality of Mother Earth, Elizabeth.
Mother Earth or Elizabeth can also help you access
the ability to heal in this physical realm.

Mother Earth,
Please be with me
as I look to access knowledge on how to heal
myself physically.
Please show me ways in which I can use herbs
or medicine
to heal myself of anything that is causing me
physical pain.
Amen

There is so much we do not know about energy or healing.
Love is an energy and it can heal.
How do we access love?
This is a difficult question
when you believe that love only exists for couples.
But why does love not exist for us as an individual?
If we can love someone else, why can we not love ourselves?

So, learning to love ourselves is an energy in itself
that can empower us to be able to heal ourselves or others.
How do we access love or the energy that love possesses?
Easily, over time, through prayer and meditation.

Dear God,
Open my world to love,
help me to see how I can love myself,
help me to see how I can empower myself,
help me to see that I have access to an energy that

can heal me,
if I can simply learn to love myself.
Amen

What is also more important as you access these gifts
and abilities
is to realize that nothing comes in this lifetime you live in
that does not have a physical price tag.
If you are looking to heal
and if you are looking to create a gift such as healing,
know that there is a certain something
you must pay back for having that gift.

The price tag may be to suddenly mature or grow up.
The rose-colored glasses come off
and you see there is also a very dark side to the reality you
live with not just a beautiful one of healing.
There is also one of sickness, death, pain, misery and
so forth and sometimes to access those abilities to heal
requires you must look at the darker side of living
which can be a physical reality
that is not necessarily beautiful.

In order to have dark, you must have light.
In order to have light, you must have darkness.

There always has to be two sides to every coin.
In order to have healing abilities
you also have to have sickness
and the list goes on and on and on.
You cannot be gifted with healing abilities
if you do not pay a price tag for it.
It just is not possible in this physical reality.

Mother Earth will assist you to pay a price tag
for what it is you are receiving.
If you are drawing on her knowledge
or her energy to heal somebody,
then there is a price to pay for that.
There is a price to pay for healing yourself.
Naivety or ignorance do not belong here.
The physical reality has a great demand attached to it.

A demand that many do not know even exists.
The reason I'm writing about healing is that
I have spent years learning to heal and learning to help others.
Do I believe this is possible?
Well, yes, it is possible.
Anything is possible if you believe,
yet everything takes time and work.

If you look at an athlete who's preparing for the Olympics,
if you speak with any of them,
they will tell you they spend countless hours, days
and months, and many times, years working to compete in those Olympics.
There is a price tag for them to endure physically
in order to rise above their physical reality of being average.
They must become exceptional athletes, exceptional at
their sport, and they must pay a price tag for it.
Often it is a hefty price tag as they will tell you,
years of being up early and working late
over and over and over and over again doing the same exercises
and all for what, just a moment in time to surpass
what they believe is possible of their physical body.

Each of you can also go beyond that without having to suffer physically,
yet, at the same time,
you must learn to teach the mind and the physical body
to go beyond this reality to see there is more
than what meets the eye to what reality you exist in.
So, to be able to access that healing energy,
you must delve deeply into the subconscious
that we have little awareness of,
and it may take years to tap that knowledge and understanding.

For those who are naturally gifted with these abilities of healing,
they perhaps can teach you more quickly how to get there.
Yet, they may not even understand how they accessed that knowledge.
It's been a gift that was given to them
that they perhaps were born with.
Some are able to teach what that gift is

and how they access the knowledge and healing energy,
which goes beyond the physical,
and is not limited by the physical,
and that is how you heal.
You go beyond what you believe is possible.
It is an energy that changes the vibration within your body
and that vibrational change heals your body.

My hope is that
each of you will be able to, with time, access the knowledge
you need to discover
what it is that you are looking for in this physical reality.

Chapter Thirteen
FORGIVENESS

Since starting this book, I've noticed that my closest friends
have become more and more excited about it
and have stepped forward to become more involved.

And I ask myself why?

It's become obvious to me as I have divulged some of the contents of this book
that it's the material that is creating excitement.

They're excited to learn more and to get to know themselves better
and to challenge themselves to rise above their circumstances in their lives
and have a great deal more fulfillment.

They not only gain more spiritual knowledge,
they also develop their intuition and insights to achieve more concrete results thereby propelling their spiritual growth forward in acquiring some of the abilities I have already obtained.

Launching this book has revived my creative side
and as a result, I foresee two, maybe three, additional books unfolding from it.
As this book gains momentum with friends collaborating to make it a reality,
I watch them explore their latent talents and discovering more about God and spirituality
and achieving what previously lay dormant within.

Painting with God has been merely one facet of expressing the love that I've received while painting.
Jesus comes to me with love, forgiveness, compassion, understanding and acceptance.
All qualities I do not yet fully grasp.
I look forward to challenging myself to forgive, heal and love at higher levels than I am accustomed to.

On this physical plain of Earth, many of us have a limited concept of forgiveness.
We believe we love but we fail to forgive,
something our parents' generation lived by –
the old rule book of 'be hard and protect yourself at all costs'.
I have lived that way throughout my life and I am paying dearly for it.
I need to learn more about how to love unconditionally.

I would love to understand on a deeper level what God wants of me.
Does God want me to forgive?
Does God want me to love freely?
I would think and hope the answer is 'yes'.
Yet, do I actually know how to achieve love?
I don't know how to truly achieve it.
I need guidance. I need love. I need to be shown how to forgive.
I need to be shown how to accept love, give love freely
and then hopefully I will be able to show others by example.

There is so much in this world to explore, define, discover and understand.
We need to grow, understand and learn.
We need to love and to care more.
We need to take care of the planet, of others, of ourselves and the people we love.
We need to learn how to be forgiving, how to be loving,
how to respect and care for one another
and to understand that we are all human, we are all frail,
we are all weak and sometimes we do not know better.

If there was more forgiveness in the world,
I wonder where my life would have led me
if I had more forgiveness, more tolerance, more acceptance,
more understanding and more compassion.
I still do not have enough compassion.
I still do not have enough forgiveness.
I hope I do not wait until it's too late to start to practice the little that I do know.
I'm sure when passing into spirit or dying I think God will be there watching

and then I think I will have to own up
to my knowing better and not trying harder.
How do you tell God that you are sorry?
I still do not have enough compassion.
I still do not have enough forgiveness.

You knew that you needed to change but you didn't.

I have also explored the brighter, more beautiful side of myself
that I have so thoroughly enjoyed.
After exploring painting, I decided to write songs and
eventually this led to the recording
and release of an album.

Writing and singing was one of the most enjoyable things I
have ever done in my life.
I had practiced only for a few years and was just learning to
play the piano.
It is phenomenal to be able to explore a creative
aspect of oneself
and get that opportunity at any time in one's life.

Music is another one of the many languages God speaks.
God speaks to us through music.
Music is as old as history, religion and man.
Music unites us as we listen, sing or play together,
we resonate together.

Music is vibrational in nature and is a medium to take us to
higher realms of learning and understanding.
Music is a form of forgiveness.
It matters not the past history or the present,
it only matters that we can all enjoy the same singer or music.

What is it that you desire to explore in your life?
Do not wait until it's too late, express it now.
Do not wait to love, do it now.
Do not wait to forgive, do it now.
Do not wait for compassion, do it now.

We may believe we have the answers
and, even though they may be the right answers,
they're rarely useful unless we practice them.

Painting with God has helped me to align my inner self
with my outer self and my higher self.
Perhaps your life too will also align.

Destiny has brought you here to me.
Explore yourself and gain more clarity as to why you are here
and what you're living for.
It doesn't have to be huge and complex. It can be a very
simple understanding.

I am leaving you with just one thought.
If you are in doubt, know that God is right there beside you.
You don't have to go searching, you can just simply say 'God
I know you are here'.

And remember the old adage 'forgive, forget and move on'.
Find the wings that will carry you to move on with love, light
and forgiveness.

Chapter Fourteen
INTRODUCTION TO THE KUNDALINI

After much deliberation and consideration,
I've decided to talk about a topic that I initially left on the shelf.
A topic that most of us know very little about,
Kundalini, and how to awaken it.

Awakening your Kundalini is something that can happen over a long period of time.
It can be a very long and slow process that can take years and years, or it can happen suddenly through a tragedy, a death, an illness, and in my case, through my spiritual development.

Eight months ago, I awakened my Kundalini energy fully.
Over the eight months, I have been incredibly emotional and anxiety ridden, a common occurrence with igniting the Kundalini.

The Kundalini is incredibly powerful and it is the energy that many healers use.
It is a gateway to God that allows us access to healing energy and power
that typically, in this physical reality, just lies dormant in the average person.
Yet, anyone who desires to awaken it and work at it can become exceptional healers.

In the past eight months based on my Kundalini experience,
I have also learned it is internal and comes with an incredibly high price tag we don't see when we initially ignite it
and we must pay to have it.

That price can appear to be expensive and out of reach,
yet, if we want abilities that go far beyond our normal horizon,
we must pay in some way.

And what payment is required?

With each person it is different.

Whereas, some might experience the awakening
of the Kundalini
as a rattling of the cage of their physical body
along with the mental and emotional turmoil.
Others may find themselves suddenly awake
with a new awareness of their life flame burning more
brightly than ever
inside a new finely tuned instrument.

At times I debated with myself whether I really awakened
my Kundalini or whether it was the Kundalini igniting itself.
Even now I am still not 100 per cent sure.

When ignited, each person goes through a different experience.
For some, it can be terrifying and for others, it can
be enlightening.
It depends on the person, their karma and what they
plan to accomplish.

Over the past eight months, the experience has brought me
closer to God,
not only painting with God but through prayer and acknowl-
edging that God is there
and that God can do so much to heal.

In addition to igniting the Kundalini,
I found myself also looking to find answers from God,
Jesus, angels and all those in spirit.

I started developing my intuition in my early twenties
and still use it now.
I became aware of the Kundalini energy
and it has gradually revealed itself to me.

Can you make a choice to ignite it?
Yes, you can, but I would recommend you use caution
because your life may take a complete turn.
It is not something that just stays stationary, your life may
become completely altered.

It's not something where you become a great deal wiser
and a great deal more mature.

One may be frightened to death of what they see
and what they are experiencing.
Due to the impact from COVID,
many people may be about to ignite their Kundalini
because they have been confined to sit around alone facing their fears,
including their fear of death.

When one feels powerless against the war and against sickness and dying,
it can spontaneously trigger the awakening of their Kundalini.

Chapter Fifteen
IGNITING THE KUNDALINI

Sometimes I hear God speaking to me though not in actual words but rather through an impression or feeling. It's not a voice speaking to me. It's a sense.

In the past five months, I have felt a strong desire and intuition to teach classes
and give people hope and purpose.
Now, I am teaching.
Teaching has rarely been the easiest thing for me,
especially when related to personal growth.

People want to do anything but learn personal growth.
Trying to teach people patience is like trying to teach sheep how to sing or how to sit and eat dinner properly.
It's just not happening.
It's quite hard to accomplish tasks that literally seem impossible.

I did pursue the classes with a passion
because I realized that God knew more than I did.
I taught classes for many years
but now I thought I'd just do what I could.
As the classes built momentum, a core group attended consistently
until it became a nightly event.

To work with one's Kundalini is a phenomenal and exceptional experience
that few ever get to achieve in a lifetime.
It is something that enhances one's ability to do many different things, but especially healing.

Many want to have this gift as Christ had this gift.
Most do not want the price tag that comes with it,
and the price tag can be simply staggering, overwhelming and too challenging to accept or deal with.
That is why the average person rarely goes after manifesting or igniting their Kundalini.

It is quite frightening to say the least.
It is overwhelming, overpowering and it is the unknown which leaves one fearful of death. The Kundalini amplifies our fears of death because it takes us into the unknown
and many of us are frightened of death and frightened of the unknown.
So, when one starts to tap their Kundalini,
they often can quickly leave it alone
simply because they sense danger and fear
and they sense death.
They become quite frightened and decide it's not for them.

So, if it is something you do decide to undertake,
be prepared to have your whole life completely and totally changed,
and not necessarily for the better.
It could then take you into a whole new awakening and awareness in your life
that you might not be prepared for.

My advice to anyone who is looking to become a healer
and to ignite their Kundalini energy,
and it would be a strong one,
is to find somebody who knows what they're doing,
knows what they're working with,
and perhaps has worked with the Kundalini
for many, many, many years, if not lifetimes.
However, I must again caution you to be well prepared
that someone might think they know what they're doing
when working with the Kundalini
and may not be fully aware of the dangers or limitations it can bring with it.

So again, do as much reading and
asking of questions before undertaking this as something
you think is just a development either intuitively or psychically.
It is not.
It is a rare gift that few have and to materialize it,
it is something that certainly can change your whole life
in a way that you may not want it changed.
Sometimes the simple average life is worth its weight in gold.

Chapter Sixteen
KUNDALINI ENERGY – GATEWAY TO GOD

There are numerous reasons why people wish to raise their Kundalini energy.

The Kundalini is the gateway to God. It is transformative.
The energy can heal one's life dramatically in a very short period of time.
It also can be enticing, charismatic,
and it can make one stand out as very charming
and desirable.

Some of those who understand what the Kundalini is
see it as something powerful.
If one wishes to establish a competitive edge,
then Kundalini is often a means to achieve that.

The Kundalini also, and this is a side note,
has a longing and a desire to work and develop with anything that is or deals with the occult.
There is a very strong desire to be much more in touch with God
or much more in touch with oneself,
much more in touch with one's intuitive, one's psychic abilities,
anything that would deal with healing, transformation,
self-discovery, self-acceptance and self-love.

The list goes on but very few people read the fine print.
Another way to look at it is that you could be looking at a year to two years to figure out how to tame that energy.
When the Kundalini is awakened, oftentimes your sexual energy rises with it.
If you were not sexually active in your youth or mid-life, or even later, you might find yourself trying to recapture that aspect of your youth.

Nothing remains the same.
All of a sudden, you're thinking differently,
seeing things differently and seeing your friends differently.

You're quickly challenged in your personal world by those around you.

Whether through your family, your siblings, your parents, your friends, everything gets turned topsy-turvy.
Be prepared to deal with your friends' or family's envy towards you.
People may get angry and they may want to get even.

You may be left asking yourself "what did I do to deserve this?".
You wanted a powerhouse in your backyard
and you got one.

Kundalini is a protector and often will protect you in ways you wouldn't expect.
You might get a strong feeling not to trust your best friend or your neighbour,
only to discover they've been deceiving you in some way.

Kundalini is like an angel watching out over you.
But can you awaken this and then walk away from life that you have known?
Not really. No one else is going to do the work for you.
That is something you must do.
You're going to work more than you normally do
because suddenly you're searching for answers
as to why you are alive, why you exist,
and what lifetimes you've come through
that have brought you into this lifetime.

Why are you here?
Do you still want to be here?
How long do you want to live?
Do you want to die?
When are people around you going to die?
Again, the questions are unending.

When you awaken the Kundalini, God becomes the center of your life
as do your guides and spirits.

Your normal life becomes boring
and you're apt to be on the move
traveling, researching, and discovering
to find out what makes others tick and what makes you tick.

You want to stay on purpose, to help people, to help
yourself more.
You want answers.

Awakening the Kundalini is about discovering answers to
your life that you never realized were there.
As you seek answers, you may wish to resolve
childhood issues.
Why didn't I like my childhood?
What did my siblings experience that I didn't?
What did I miss?

You may desire a move to a different country.
For example, you may want to stay at an ashram in India
and study yoga for two years.
That is what happens when you awaken the Kundalini.

Will awakening the Kundalini make you want money?
Highly unlikely. If anything, you may want to give your
money away
because you've come to the realization it's just a distraction.
It's not going to make you happy.
If anything, it may be making you miserable.

Many people may become attracted to you.
You may find you have new people hanging around
that never bothered with you before you awakened.

When the Kundalini awakens, you may view your life
as mundane and boring, and you may want out.
You are drawn to live a life of exuberance
full of challenges and excitement.

You may want to take action towards living life to the fullest.
You might enroll in courses to learn sign language
or do volunteer work or get behind a charity cause that can
use your help.

Or simply enjoy a minimum-wage job at McDonald's on the corner and getting to relive your youth.

Another effect of the Kundalini energy is to make you feel younger.
It will make you think and look younger.
It will give you boundless energy.
You might stay up all night working on a project
and feel totally energetic to go to work the next day
without missing a single beat.

More energy also means more healing energy.
With all of that healing energy,
you may find rebuilding a healthier body through exercise
and seeking out healthier ways to eat.

Along with awakening the Kundalini comes the desire for longevity.
It may also bring out a lifelong desire to learn and teach yoga.
You might become inspired to become a marathon runner.

Kundalini likes movement
and suddenly you also like a lot of movement.
You become an "Energizer Bunny". You like to be on the go.
There will be different places you want to go and want to see
because you're charged up and ready to go.

Awakening the Kundalini is also of great value
for those already in the occult such as psychics or healers.
Kundalini increases your ability to heal
and get in touch with your physical body and what it needs.

You may feel a great deal of heat in your body
up and down your spine.
You may find yourself often feeling restless,
needy or fearful of abandonment.

Igniting the Kundalini is like opening Pandora's Box.
Rarely does it awaken the things that make you feel
good or safe because it is all about change.
It's not about resting, not about laying back

and being at peace, just the opposite.
If you wish to awaken the Kundalini, be prepared for a
lot of change
and, initially, change you may not like a whole lot.
But in a year or two, you could be very thankful that you did.

Upon awakening the Kundalini, I've been much
more creative,
much more aware of others around me and the games
people play.

I've also been more aware of my desires
and of what I want to accomplish before I die.
The Kundalini's awakening also brings up issues
around death.

Not just your death, but anyone close to you,
family, friends and distant relatives.

Death and death issues will be front and center.
The need to know, to learn and to see will
become paramount.

Chapter Seventeen
YOU CAN BE YOUNG

I did a good deal of thinking around COVID and
how it has affected me and how I've responded.
I believe that the future will be about humanity finding God
and finding ourselves in the quiet moments.

There were so many beautiful title choices for this book that
I considered, before choosing 'Painting with God'.
I could have called this book 'My time with God', 'Speaking
with God', 'Knowing God', 'Loving God' or 'Coming to Embrace God'.

But 'Painting with God' is my language with God.

COVID has isolated all of us from the world we once knew
from our loved ones and from ourselves.

We no longer feel free to wander out and drop in spontaneously visiting brothers, sisters and relatives very easily.
We may feel imprisoned in our lives which, of course, can be
emotionally horrific for many of us who have never felt such
level of isolation before.

Some of us have found our personal lives have been
literally destroyed.
Friendships have been kept distant,
and we can no longer invite five, six or seven people over to
gather and chat and laugh
without risking being perceived as careless by
our neighbours.

Suddenly, everyone has become a likely possibility of
greeting death at our door
and many of us have taken to isolating ourselves
and avoiding people who we would casually interact with
in the past.

Do I see myself going back to a normal life ever again?
I sense a resounding "No", most likely for another two to
three years.

Even if within that time period life returns to some resemblance of what used to be,
I don't think I could call it normal.

A better question might be "what will normal look like?".
Even before COVID, I don't think I realized I had somewhat of a normal life.
Now, I certainly see that my life is not normal.

Nowadays, going to the store to get groceries represents my outing and my socializing event for the day.
It has become one of the rare occasions where I get to see people.

Jumping into the car for a simple drive can be an outing.
I am probably more fortunate than some, fortunate enough to socialize every day with people.
This for me is a lifesaver in many respects.

I chose to teach classes on Kundalini in order to assist my friends who wanted to heal themselves and those close to them.

Many of us may not recognize that COVID measures and restrictions are causing a mass scale of undetected depression in the population at large.
Many of us are unaware we ourselves may be experiencing depression, thus, looking for ways out
with very few options available.

Some have coped by taking up new hobbies such as crafts and music.
Others have taken to get their bodies into better shape with improved diets and yoga.

The more we sit with it, the more difficult it becomes.
If the development of your intuition is still green
or you are normally a socially active individual,
developing your Kundalini can be a way to alleviate some of the stress.
Your newly found strength gives you purpose to
move forward.

It was God calling out to me in early spring that said “teach”. God inspired me to give people hope and to develop spiritually. I approached my long-standing friends with the idea for the classes and surprisingly they were all open to further discover themselves.

From there the class grew enough to balance
the Kundalini sessions to make learning and awareness
much more enjoyable.

Now well into the fall, I’m finding my own Kundalini is
healing me and moving me forward in ways I wasn’t expecting
before.

The Kundalini is a way to get closer to God
and to your own divine power and energy.
It is a way to experience your soul in its brightest light and
fullest potential.

One who is very religious in the traditional sense might see
this as blasphemous.
“There is only God.”
Well, believe it or not, we’re all a part of God.
We have that speck of light within us that belongs to God
and when we allow it to shine brightly, we can’t help but
see God.

There is an opportunity in that speck of light, within our soul,
within the heart of who we are is the Kundalini,
a spark of God energy,
expressing in this physical plane through our bodies.
As we tap that little speck of light deep within our soul,
the power within it is immeasurable.
We can reach out to the God that we might only believe
is residing outside of ourselves, beyond the clouds or in spirit,
where we have not yet gone.

The isolation can also be seen as an opportunity for us to
breathe in God,
for us to know the universe,
for us to know the angels in heaven in spirit,
for us to know the lifetimes that we’ve journeyed through to
get here and the experiences we’ve all had.

COVID is not our first disease, not for any of us.
This is just a small little smidgen of our cumulative experiences in past lives.
Many of us have traveled through many a lifetime and probably lived through or died with the plague and other diseases that would completely wipe out entire villages.

How many times have we experienced, war, religions, and God?

Many of us have traveled through Atlantis,
supposedly a mystical place from long, long ago,
but as I connect with my own Akashic records,
I see myself as having been a phenomenal healer using light to heal others.

Where does that light come from, I am not certain
but I recognize that in this life,
I have once again tapped into that light within me that I use to heal.

Just to be clear, this is not about advising anyone
not to seek out the medical profession if you are sick.
If you are sick or injured, go to your doctor
or through the medical channels to alleviate your suffering.

This is simply another avenue of healing, another option.
This is an alternative so you may find and connect with the light within you,
the energy within you that does the healing.

Will it heal you?
I am uncertain as that's between you and God
but it is an option, very worthwhile exploring.
These books I am doing are not simply out of the blue.
They represent the years of hard work I have gone through
in order to accomplish and to have this kind of wisdom
and insight.
I spent 30 years developing my Kundalini, my intuition and my psychic abilities.
This is not something that has come to me overnight.

I can then speak to you and offer you insights regarding your own development,
if that is something you so desire.

There are so many options available in this world that we are unaware of.
At this stage in my life, as I age and my youth gradually dwindles each year,
when I look in the mirror, I still see a young man.

Those around me see someone who is at least 10 or 15 years younger,
sometimes even more, which sometimes still surprises me.
But at the same time, it doesn't surprise the young man that lives within me
who says "yes, you are still young".

Can you stay young?
Yes, you can stay young by tapping the energy within you.
When you tap that Kundalini healing energy, that God energy, it can renew your youth.
It can bring you back to the life you once knew.
You can find yourself a great deal healthier if you choose.

Is it ever too late?
Never.

If you choose God,
if you choose the Dancing Angels,
if you choose Jesus to heal and guide you, along with Michael the Archangel,
to show you and light your path, you'll soon realize
that youth does not have an age.
It does not have a timeline.
You can be young until you are 90.
Your body can stay relatively young and healthy until you are 85 to 90
if you choose to work with your body, food, meditating and yoga.
All these different options are open to you.

Youth is available and you do not have to go out to a store to buy it.
Practice it. Believe it. Pray.
Acknowledge the God before you
and become a humble servant.

Ask the voice of God to speak within you to show you what is possible
and what miracles can happen.
You are a miracle in this world.
We are all miracles.

Be the miracle you've always believed you could be.
Take the opportunity, regardless of your age,
whether you're a baby boomer or millennial,
or whatever you are, be something exceptional.
Take your health in your hands and work with it
and work with the God you know exists in you
and watch what unfolds before you.

The options are endless.
Find a friend who you can discuss this with.
Talk about what your goals are.

If you are retired and you've never traveled to Europe
and you've always dreamed of backpacking,
what better time than now to get out and start hiking.

By spring, throw a knapsack on your back,
throw your phone in your bag,
put on your hiking boots and get out and go.
Be that young person you have always wanted to be
and refuse to be somebody else.

Take the opportunity to recognize that the age you feel is a reflection of what you feel inside about yourself, not your neighbour nor your friends.

You're saying, "I can't."
No one else is saying you can't.
You're saying you can't.

There are people out there looking for these opportunities.
Go online and Google 'Opportunities - Hiking and Backpacking through Europe',
'Train riding through Europe', 'Passenger passes for rail through Europe', to name just a few.

Don't let your youth slip away without a fight.
Fight it.
Fight it.
Take hold of your world and make these things happen.
Make your youth possible.
If you are terrified to do this, then live in your fear.
Face your fear and live through it – it is only temporary.

Do not let fear win. Do not let COVID win.
You can win. You can be young. You can be healthy.

If you want to travel,
then go out and get a vaccine shot,
throw your phone in your knapsack,
put on your hiking boots and get moving.
If you do not wish to take the vaccine shot,
then backpack locally.

Take a risk. Take chances. God is a risk.
When you start communicating to God
and looking for signs that God is talking back to you,
you are then in touch with your intuition.

You are in touch with that speck of light that resides within you that I call God.
Let yourself get back in touch with the God you know.
Don't let age rob you of your youth
just because you believe this happens to everyone who reaches a certain number.
It doesn't happen to everybody.
It happens to those who let it happen.

Will your body remain youthful and healthy even if you consume alcohol regularly?
No.
If you are overeating, will your body stay young and healthy?

No.
Why won't it? You are abusing your body and preventing the flow of Kundalini.
You cannot abuse your body and expect it will stay young and vibrant for you.

Keep young and vibrant by eating well and exercising daily.
If you want to drink, then drink water.
If you poison your body with alcohol, then expect consequences.
Those consequences are not something you are going to enjoy when you are in the hospital at 70 or 80 asking yourself where you took the wrong turn.

Now is the time to choose which way to turn and change your life.
If you smoke, stop smoking.
It is a proven indicator that if you smoke, you are more likely to end up with cancer at some point in time.
If you haven't yet and you're smoking, butt it out and take a close look at your life.

Bring the youth and your health back in and pray to God that you know and see how you can make yourself healthy again.

Do I sound preachy as I'm writing this?
Of course I sound preachy.
In my youth, I had my time of drinking, smoking and doing damage to my body.
I am no longer doing that to my body so, I can say to each of you find a way out.
Find a healthy way out.

You can be 90 and still out hiking and even climbing Mount Everest if you are still healthy.
Face your fears and know you can choose to stay youthful up until the day you die.
You can have friends until the day you die.
You can have family with you until the day you die.
You don't have to die alone.

You don't have to die in a retirement home.
You don't 'have to'.
These choices are often forced upon us in society because we believe that they're the only option.
They're not the only option.

Why can you not find friends to live with until the day you die?
Why does it have to be a retirement home? It doesn't have to be.
Those are options that have been cut out of our lives because we believe we are aging and there is no choice.

There are always choices.
There are always options.

It is up to you to discover what those options are.
Create them, make a new path and find a new way to live.
Just because everyone else is living the old way doesn't mean you 'have to'.
Create a new path. Your path.

America was once noted as the land of the free.
Well, if it's the land of the free, then it still is the land of the free, free choice.
You have choice. You can choose. You can and maybe you will choose a different path.

Maybe you will die younger, maybe you won't live past 70 or maybe you won't live past 80, but at least you can choose up until then
and do things that you are going to enjoy doing.

Break free, break out.
If COVID has you restricted, then go and get yourself vaccinated
so that you can at least wander the streets freely and without fear.

If a new strain of the virus takes you down, then so be it, at least you will go down fighting.
Fight is my word to each of you.
Fight to be a part of the God that you do not know even exists.

There is a God within you so let it out, be a part of that God, get in touch with that God and get in touch with youth.

You are not going to find youth in a book, you are going to find it within you.
Youth resides within you. You can stay young if you decide to stay young.
Choose youth.

If you are able, get out and walk every day
and breathe in deeply all the fresh air you can no matter what the weather.
Get out every day and stay youthful.

Today as I paint with God, within my energy, I thank God for giving me the voice and to pass this message onto you, to break out and to be free.

May God speed you to your destiny.

Chapter Eighteen
PAINTING HEAVEN

How do you paint heaven?
We all have our unique version of heaven
just as we all have different visions of love.

What is love? Who is love? Is God love?
Has God created an Angel of Love?

There are many angels who carry the love vibration
just as there are many humans who carry love vibrations.
When you are seeking love in life, when you are
seeking a partner,
seek not someone who can give you love
but rather seek someone who will always be there with you,
through all the ups and downs and all the storms,
all the good times and the difficult times.

Seek out someone who is consistent, patient, caring
and understanding.
If you can find that, then you have defined love and you have
painted heaven.

Heaven is not about living in bliss all the time.
Heaven is about knowing who you are,
knowing where you're going and living in peace while
you do it.
For most of my life I've sought out love.
Secretly, in my own thoughts, I think it is still there, though
sometimes I deny it.

What did I look for?
All the wrong things as most of us have at one time
or another.

Love was always fast and happy with lots of energy.
I fooled myself numerous times into thinking I was in love
with someone who turned out to not even know I existed.

How could someone else love me when I didn't know what love was nor did I know how to like myself, respect myself or care about myself.
I never demanded of someone else
that they respect me, love me, care for me or be there for me.

Now, I see love much differently.
Age, time and wisdom have helped me to see
that love is something that requires patience, understanding, compassion and empathy.

Love is about staying with someone through the good times and the bad times.
Love isn't happy ever after.
Love isn't Cinderella or Snow White.
Love is about staying the course through
all the ups and all the downs
and knowing that you enjoy doing it
because you care about the person
and wish to explore the limits of love with them.

When you are out there looking for love, do not look hard.
Who do you like? Who do you get along with?
Who enjoys your company as much as you enjoy theirs?
These are the simple things that give you indicators towards love.

That is what you're really looking for,
the person who enjoys your company,
the person who wants to be with you.

You're not looking for the person who wants to like you for your looks or your money.
Attract someone who likes you the way you are
and likes to be with you and sharing time with you.

Let's not overlook we live in a world that is challenged greatly with pain, battles and obstacles and heavy burdens to carry.
If you are looking to go through life with someone,
you don't want somebody who's going to run off
the minute things get difficult.

What a magnificent thought,
to believe that love is something that can be that well defined,
that love can be something that cares about you,
and that you care about you, which makes it twice as strong.

So, when you get up in the morning, and when you are looking,
don't look for what you may have looked for in the past,
look for someone who will be there by your side and who
enjoys being there by your side.

Well, that may be a friend or it may not be a friend.
Keep in mind, oftentimes friends do not tell you that secretly
they're attracted to you.
Friends are there because they want to be there
and they want to spend time with you. So, friends are some-
times the best to consider for a love relationship.

You may not know your friends as well as you think you do.
Look at your friend and ask yourself:
"Do they find you attractive?
Do they like you more than they let on?
Have they been there consistently for you when things have
gone south?".

If your answer is yes,
perhaps you have found love.

Chapter Nineteen
TOUCHED BY GOD

What is it that I hope to achieve in writing this book?
I found writing this book has been quite cathartic in several ways.
It has solidified within me the conviction that God is always with me.
My inner voice is connected with God and is now connected with you.
That voice is one that resonates for me.

The years of work towards spiritual growth has taught me how much I love growing emotionally and spiritually.
It's shown me I have a gift and an ability worth sharing with those who will listen, who want to see, and want to learn and know.

I have reconnected with old friends.
It has been something that has really assisted me to grow.
Through their collaboration in publishing this book, it has shown me how committed some people can be towards their own personal growth.

Painting with God has enabled me to express a latent part of myself.
I'm now at a point where it has gone well beyond what I expected it to.
It has taught me a great deal. It has shown me a great deal.
I am still learning. I am excited about the prayers and the insights.

I was reading one of the prayers yesterday and was deeply touched.
I see the prayers in this book are an avenue for others to grow and to learn how to connect with God, Jesus or with angels and how to express oneself when one has troubles or difficulties that God, Angels, Christ, and Mother Mary are just a voice away.

Dear God,
Please help me.
Please lift this burden from my shoulders.
Help me to grow strong.
Please give me of Your strength.
Show me compassion, understanding, acceptance and love.
Please help me to be able to love and forgive.
Amen

It seems that throughout this book I've learned much about my friends.
I've come to understand who has been there, who has supported me,
who has given me so much of their time and made Painting with God possible.
Many of you are growing spiritually, learning and wanting to expand to see different parts of yourself.

COVID has restricted so many of us in every nation
and could make us feel like we weren't growing or expanding.
You can grow and expand no matter how limited the access to others is.
We grow within ourselves. We grow with just talking to God.

Every morning upon waking I sense growth from the day before.
My prayers are expanding
and my thoughts are expanding.
I'm becoming more and more linked with the thought of doing a series of books
to help others to become more in touch with their inner voices and with their God.

My teaching is growing.
It's the side of me that wants to share with you the many things I have learned over the years,
the writing, the teaching, working with spirit
and yes, working with God,
are my most cherished times as I felt so completely fulfilled in my life.

You utilize these tools to access your own voice, your own God and you may also believe you have a book in you that you want to share.
Or perhaps write about your connection with God or spirits that you want to express and share with the world.
To me, that tells me we're all connected in one form or another. We are all connected with one voice.

I do not know what my future holds for me no more than I knew what this year held for me.
2021 was an incredibly challenging year
where I have been tested beyond what I ever thought I would be tested in my life.
I found myself aging, growing, coming face to face with all of my demons and my fears
while standing back and asking myself, "why?".

Why did this happen to me?
Why did I not see this?
How could I not have known this was coming?
I did not know. I did not see.

Eight months ago, I had no idea I was going to do this book, 'Painting with God',
because it has more been in my past than in my present.
Two years ago, if you had asked me does God exist,
I would have replied with "just look around you"
or "God has come to me and God has spoken to me".
There was no doubt in my mind that God existed.

Even with the difficulties I faced this year,
even through all of that, I still would have said "Yes, God does exist".

No matter what happens to me, God does exist.
I know God is there.

Regardless of whether I die or live, God is there with me.
I may not understand God's purpose or methods to teach me but I do know that God has come to me unexpectedly and blessed and touched me in ways that I never dreamed of.

Know that God can come to you.
God can touch you when you are least expecting it.
Ask God to touch you.
Ask God to make your voice stronger.
Ask God for more sight.
I've often asked God please let me see the world through your eyes.
Let me see others through your eyes.
I see through asking that there is so much I do not know or understand.

If I turn to God and if I trust and if I believe, then so much can happen with that.
I woke up to this affirmation.

> *"I am learning to trust and believe in God.*
> *God is with me.*
> *My fears are falling away."*

That was transformative as I saw the possibilities to still grow.
There are still avenues that God can assist and help me along my path.
And for that I am incredibly grateful.

Chapter Twenty
HARNESSING THE KUNDALINI

What is it about healing that makes us all avoid it until we need it?
Typically, until we are sick, we take healing or energy for granted.
Once we're sick, then all of a sudden, the world stops for us and everything focuses on healing.
Who is it that we decide to draw in who will help us and rejuvenate us?
How do we mend a challenge each of us faces within our lives?
What are the avenues open to us?

With diseases rampant as it is today with COVID and with cancer,
there are so many different diseases that we are all trying to heal.
We are all trying to figure out how or what is the road back to our youth, to health, to what perhaps we never thought we would leave.
As we age, our main concern is health and the loss of youth.
There is one path that will bring you more youth, more energy, more healing and it is something everyone typically avoids until they have to and that is healing energy from within or even healing energy from another.

The healing profession or those who possess energy to heal pretty much have been underground for quite a number of years.
Yet, today you hear more and more about healing energy.
We hear more and more about God.
We hear more and more about the possession of youth.

One of the best avenues for healing,
and this is just my opinion from what I have found with my own health and the experiences I have had with healers,
has been igniting the flame within the Kundalini,
the healing energy within.
And that has been something that certainly has brought me

a great deal of peace of mind as I've aged
and that continues to bring me peace of mind.

For years, I have taught classes on personal growth
and energy, and how to develop it.
Now at this stage of my life, I am finding there are many
more individuals who want to access this healing energy
called the Kundalini.
People seem to know very little about it,
its power source, the depth of the energy or the depth of
the healing.

Yet, let me say this, from what I know,
it is an incredibly powerful tool that can heal
within days, sometimes weeks, sometimes even minutes,
depending on the person and how gifted they are.
Some people have a natural gift with healing energy.
It is something they are born with
just as one is born with intelligence or quick wit or charm.
One can be born with healing energy also.

My suggestion to all of you in these difficult times of COVID
and other diseases is perhaps look beyond what you're used
to for healing or for finding ways of perhaps giving yourself
peace of mind.
Again, this is something of my own personal view.
This is not something I believe everybody needs to do or has
to do or should do.
This is a personal choice.
It's a personal choice that I started when I was in my twenties
as I started to develop my intuition.
My intuition certainly has been something that has given me
a great deal of resources which has been available to me
over the years.
It still is something that I utilize on a daily basis.

This book, Painting with God, is also something
that gives one the thought that God has come to
me creatively.
God can come to one on so many different levels,
creatively, physically, emotionally and spiritually.

There are so many different avenues for God to touch each of us.
The choice is up to you on how you want God to touch you.
How do you want God to be there for you?
Do you want God to come to you with compassion, empathy, understanding, intelligence, gifts of insight and to help others to fulfill their choices in life, their destiny?
What is it that you have been sent here for?
What is it that you are here to accomplish?
There is so much more than what we realize that we can accomplish.

There is a tremendous amount available at our fingertips to us which is why I am writing this book.
It is to more inform each of you of some of the avenues I have discovered.
There are other resources you can tap and other resources you can have.
The Kundalini is something that is supposedly a very powerful healing tool.
Yet, at the same time, it is not something that is easily harnessed and that is what I would like to talk about, how to harness the Kundalini?

First to access your Kundalini, begin with a prayer:

Dear God,
Within me God is Your light.
Within me God is Your healing energy that moves silently.
I pray You allow me to access this healing energy,
if it be Your will and right for me.
I pray You help me to release that which is in me,
that which can heal,
that which can come forward
and help myself or others if I so choose.
Amen

Prayer is just one way of accessing the Kundalini.
The Kundalini can sometimes be accessed

through meditation, through chanting, through yoga,
through trauma or through death of someone close to you.
The shock or trauma can kindle the awakening.
One might experience something traumatizing
and then find that they have access to a deeper part
of themselves that they find astounding.
What's accessing it?
How do you understand it?
How do you calm it?
How do you turn it on and how do you turn it off?
Well, if you've turned it on with a prayer,
then you can turn it off with a prayer.
If you've turned it on with meditation,
then you can turn it off with meditation.
If God allows you to access this,
then God will also allow you to shut it off with the
following prayer:

Dear God,
I pray to the light within me.
I pray to know that I can shut this light off,
this energy source off
and I can become calm through any storm.
Amen

Keep in mind that if you are shutting it off
you might be shutting off the flow of energy.

If the Kundalini is something that stirs your emotions,
then perhaps your emotions need healing.
So, if you find your emotions are rampant
and upsetting with the Kundalini, then say a simple prayer:

Dear God,
These waters I am experiencing emotionally are rough.
I am finding myself unable to calm myself emotionally.
I am finding myself unable to calm this Kundalini
energy within me that heals.
I pray Dear God that You help me to calm the light.
I pray that You help me to know that I am fine,

that I am at one with You and, if I am with You,
I am safe.
Amen

And say the affirmation:

I am safe with God at all times.
My healing energy is quieting.
I am safe with myself at all times and with God.
I have nothing to fear with God.
God only wants what is best for me and for those that I love.
I pray to know that I am safe at all times.

And so, that is what the Kundalini is like.
It's like a storm.
It can be disruptive.
When you think it has to heal,
however, something is disrupting your body or your thoughts,
then the energy must be strong.

God's energy has to be strong to penetrate your fears and your worries and so much of calming this energy is about learning to trust God, learning to love God, learning to know that God is there to look out for you and that God will calm the storm.
Patience is a crucial part of tapping the resource of the Kundalini.
It takes time to sit and wait patiently for it to pass,
or for the storm to pass,
or to learn to trust that God is there listening and helping.

The lesson with the Kundalini and igniting it is learning peace and calm amidst the storm.
When others are confused or upset,
you must be willing to stay the course.
You must be willing to know you are fine no matter what.
You must know that this energy is not there to harm you but there to heal you.

Chapter Twenty-One
HEALING PRAYER

This prayer is:

*Dear God,
I ask with Your healing energy,
and the healing energy of all the souls around me,
Archangels Michael, Raphael,
and Uriel, Mother Mary and Jesus,
that You help me accept their love
and healing energy.*

*I pray as they draw close to me Dear God
that You help me to receive
their energy and love as a gift.*

*I pray from the bottom of my feet
to the top of my head that in this moment
I understand and know Your love.*

*Allow me access to Your divine love
and the healing energy
that is bestowed upon me
through Your love and light
and that I willingly and knowingly
understand the healing
that comes with Your love and light.*

*Accept this humble prayer
from a humble servant of Yours,
that I be healed,
that I come to understand Dear Lord
that the power of Your love
is beyond all things physical
and there is nothing
that is impossible to You.*

Lift the burdens from my shoulders
and help me to see
that Your love and healing energy
is infinite and limitless.
Help me to see this through Your eyes.
Help me to know beyond a shadow of a doubt
there is nothing You cannot do if You so will it.

I pray that in my one weakness of disbelief
You help me to believe
that You take me beyond the limits and boundaries
of what I have grown up with
and show me without a doubt
they're just beliefs that no longer serve me.

Nothing can stop or block Your healing energy
or Your love or Your light.

Let Your light filter into my body,
into my thoughts, into my heart, and into my soul
and help to release all the negativity that I hold
so that I may see Your love and light.

Help me to see more clearly Your love and light.
Let me know again Your love and light are stronger
than I shall ever be and Your love and light is eternal.

I pray from my limited lifetimes and knowledge
that You help me to allow in this light of love
and healing.

I pray as I receive the light and healing energy,
I recognize that I am safe on my path
and that my health, if weak, shall improve
and that my enemies, if any, shall fall away
at the sight of Your love and light.

I know now God as I speak that You are
listening to me.
I can feel it in my heart. I can feel it in my soul.
I know that You are here.

I pray Dear God that I be forgiven for all the
pain and hurt
I have caused those in my life through my ignorance.
Please help these people to see I love them
and ask for their forgiveness
and I meant no harm
nor hurt emotionally or physically.

As I am praying on my knees here before You,
I pray that with
the Archangels Michael, Raphael and
Uriel, Christ and Mother Mary
and all the other angels at Your command,
to know You are here to assist me
and to take me beyond my limited capacity.

I ask this in Your name, love and light.
Amen

Chapter Twenty-Two
EXPRESS YOURSELF

I found with aging and coming into my own,
the greatest influence on my spiritual development was God creatively showing me the numerous possibilities of what I was capable of.

You are also capable of so much more
than what you realize your potential to be.
Perhaps you've always wanted to be a singer but never let yourself be.
Maybe that is something you need to explore or perhaps write music, create a film, act or write a novel.
There are numerous, numerous possibilities.

As a woman, you might dream of becoming a race car driver
but are held back to believe it's not for you,
but maybe it is for you and exactly what you need to do.
Or you dream of being a mechanic
but you might believe that it is not a profession
that would support your chosen lifestyle.
Why not?
Why can't you be a mechanic or an architect?
Why can't you sing and produce music?
Why can't you be an Olympic star or an athlete
if that's your burning desire?
These are just a few examples of creative
expressions of God.

Do what makes you happiest.
If you want to own a house,
then become a real estate agent
and learn how to buy one.
Learn the possibilities.
If you want to be a movie star,
there are no limits to age.
If you want to be a script writer, then write scripts.
If you want to dream, then dream big.
Follow your passion, follow God home.

If you can dream it,
you can have it,
you can hold it
and you can run with it.

Dreams aren't just for the young.
Dreams are for everyone.

To paint with God, live with God, breathe with God,
eat with God
and know God wants you to be the best you can be
at whatever you choose to be.

Let yourself be dynamic.
Let yourself be the superstar you want to be in your mind,
and in your heart and your soul.

Maybe you won't achieve outward recognition
and you don't have to achieve it outwardly.
Not everyone needs to know you're a superstar.

Become your own superstar.
Be the best you can be.

Break out of prison.
Break out of what confines you to your world
and find a different world.
Create it and know that God will help you to create it.

Express yourself.
Find your voice.
If you're a nurse and you want to be a doctor, become a doctor.
If you're a dental hygienist and you want to be a dentist, become a dentist.

If you fear being old and frail, embrace youth.
Surround yourself with youth and become youthful.
Find your legs, your arms, your breath,
and swim, walk, exercise and bike.

Do what you need
to stay young and fit.

Do what you need
to be the best you can be at
whatever age you are.

And the heart is where the passion is.
The more in tune you become with your heart,
the more passionate you will become.
The more passionate you become,
the more likely you are to follow your dreams.

I spent most of my life,
even from a young age,
doing two things.
First and foremost,
I chased my dreams
and believed I could achieve them.

Secondly, I chased love
everywhere I went.
I've been disappointed.
I've been walked away from.
Yet, there is a part of me
that still seeks love.
Why?
Because I love a challenge.
I love that love does not want me yet
and so I chase it.
I laugh with it. I run after it.
Even if it won't let me catch it,
I don't have to catch it to love.

Loving love is about what life is about.
It's an adventure.
When you paint with God in your life,
everything becomes an adventure.
You dream bigger
than you could possibly imagine.
Let yourself dream.
If you fail, then fail
and write about it or sing about it.
When you fail, you can say to yourself
"at least I lived my life."

I lived and I dreamed with God.
We laughed together,
we loved together
and we had fun together.

I love loving God.
I love believing in God because God believes in me
and together we can run free through life and laugh.

God wants you to laugh.
God wants you to try everything you want to try
that is healthy and good for you.
If it isn't healthy and good for you
then I don't think you want it
and I don't think God wants it for you.

If you've always wanted to travel,
then pack a backpack, get out your thumb and go to Europe
and travel.
Meet people, laugh, learn, live, love, breathe and
see the world.

I don't care if there's never anyone else there.
God is enough for me.
God fills my life in more ways than I could possibly tell you.

God makes sure I have enough of all the things I need,
the dreams I want to dream, the things I desire to laugh about
and all I need to know about spirituality.
I trust the path I am on.

What is it about painting with God that excites me?
God makes me passionate about painting.
I love colour and I love creating.

I love knowing God is here with me with everything I do when
I paint.
One morning God came to sit at
the foot of my bed
and since that morning
it has been nothing but my being impressed
with beautiful wonderful thoughts
to paint.

I know God is here with me when I sleep and when I'm awake.
God is here when I'm sad or depressed and walks with me and listens to me.
God listens and loves me regardless of where I am, regardless of the pain that I am enduring.

I have shared with you many prayers
to help you seek out your gifts
by expressing yourself through prayer.

Here is a prayer to ask God
to help you to develop your intuition:

Dear God,
As I am capable
as anyone of having a strong intuition
where guides and teachers
in spirit can speak to me,
whisper things to me,
impress me with images
and make me more
knowledgeable and more insightful.
I desire to have that gift God.

I ask You to help me to develop
my intuition and my psychic abilities
and bring a teacher to me if I need one.
Help me to open my eyes
when they're there.
Let myself be taught.
Help me to be taught
how to be everything
I don't realize I am.
With time we will sing together.
It may be silently
or it may be out loud.

Thank You God
for opening these doors and windows in my house
and helping me to shout out "I love You".
Come in and spend time with me.
I know that is what You are all about,
letting me
come to my fullest potential and expression.
And I pray You will paint with me in my life
and help me to create
a beautiful jigsaw puzzle of colour and brilliance.
As I paint, I pray You will show me
how to make it sensational.
I pray You show me
how to be sensational.
I pray You help me to see
that I can heal myself and others
if I so desire.
I can be intuitive
and use that intuition in all areas of my life.
I pray now for those
who are around me
and I wish them all the best
with Your love, light and energy.
Thank you.
Amen

Chapter Twenty-Three
FINDING YOUR VOICE

My painting and the inspiration that I received from God
has led me into the music world
of using my voice as an instrument.

My first album is on iTunes and Spotify,
and includes the songs 'Superman Kissed Me'
and 'I'm a Cowboy in My Dreams'.

I am presently working on my second album
while writing this book.
One of the new songs is 'Angels Fall'.
I can't begin to tell you how happy I am
to be singing again.

I began singing lessons a few years ago.
I didn't take them because I was expecting a finished product.
I took them for myself
and to prove to myself that I could sing if I wanted to.

When I first heard myself sing, I squirmed and cringed.
But over time, and with years of work,
my voice began to change and became an instrument.

Whether you're writing, taking a motor out of a car
or learning to play the trombone or violin,
do not stop yourself from being an instrument of God.

Let God flow through you and
give yourself the permission to embrace God.
Give yourself permission to sing and dance with the angels.
Let your heart paint with God.
Let your heart be your instrument
to guide you over the open sea, the vast forest or
the quiet desert.

These past eight months
have been probably the most challenging
and difficult time in my life
but also incredibly rewarding.

I learned so much about God,
my capabilities and strengths
as I weathered some incredibly
dark, difficult and depressing periods
helping me to more clearly understand
what people go through
when they are challenged in life.

I now understand what COVID can do to people
and the stress of being repressed and confined can
do to one.
The doors have been opened to my understanding
so much more about myself and others.

We have better insight into what others go through
when we too are challenged in a similar way.

Recognize even though COVID has kept us confined,
it may also have done the opposite and liberated us inwardly.

Look inwardly to see why you believe you are suffering
and learn what God is teaching you
for God is teaching us our lessons.

Take every dark cloud and find the silver lining
as that silver lining could be God's thread.
Find God in everything you do
including anything you might perceive as suffering.

When you see those around you who are also suffering,
you are better prepared to empathize and respect their journey
and understand and accept them through kindness.
This is God's language.

We can then understand why lifetime after lifetime we come
here to suffer.
At some point in life, we all suffer, sometimes great and diffi-
cult pain.
Sometimes we are not able to weather the storms
and we succumb to them.
Yet, perhaps that was our destiny.

In the past eight months with all my challenges,
I often wondered whether I could endure
all the difficulties and the challenges
but I still faced them and kept going.

As I learned with each passing day,
I always have something to be thankful for.

I have a life. I have a reason.
I have friends. I have family.
I have a voice that God has given me.

Do not be afraid to find your voice to call to God
and ask for assistance, or through Dancing Angels or guides,
who come to stand by your side and walk with you.
Listen to your inner voice and connect with your heart.
Connect with your spirit guides.
Connect with everyone and anyone
who assists you to learn and grow.

And growing and learning, from my experience, can be incredibly painful.
However, when you come out on the other side, God is always there with a gift for you when you graduate from the lessons you needed to learn.

I have so enjoyed sharing my thoughts
and experiences and the prayers
that have been summoned
from my heart and soul.

For the challenges I have met continuously over the past eight months,
I have called upon God endlessly
to lift the burdens from my shoulders
and take me by the hand and guide me along the path.
And God so graciously has done just that,
very slowly I thought at first,
but as time passed, I realized I was learning patience.

I've never known patience in my life.
Now I've had to learn it.

It has been at such a phenomenal cost.
Yet, in God's wisdom and sight,
we may know not why we must endure storms.
We only know afterwards
what gifts and spices
will be delivered on that ship
that makes it to port.

I pray that in the coming months
God gives me more prayers to share with you
as an ever-endless flow of inspiration and
as a beacon of light to guide you through your storms.

May these prayers lift you up,
inspire you and brighten your heart and life
in the same way they have brightened mine.

I would like to give you a prayer
to pass on to God for all the blessings
I have been given in these past number of months:

Dear God,
I come to You today
with an abundance of gratitude
for inspiring me and keeping me safe along my difficult journey.
I thank You for releasing me from my fears
and protecting me.

I thank You for the endless wonder
that You bring into my life,
for all that You inspire in me
and the beautiful kind people
that surrounded me.

I thank You for showing me all the paths
that lead to Your door,
for showing me the healing light with the Kundalini and
for helping me to teach others how to heal

while learning to heal myself.
I thank You for the endless gifts of art
that You have given to me
and for allowing me to share it with others.
I thank You for helping me to paint each stroke
and for using the palette with Your hands
guiding mine.

I thank You for Your silent voice that said to me:
"I am with you, little one, every step of the way,
I am with you, little one, you have nothing to fear
for I will bring you home safely".

I thank You for bringing me home safely
when I had my doubts that I would make it.
The sun came out and I returned with the sun
on my face
and the wind at my back.

I cannot begin to thank You enough
for helping me to see how fortunate I am
to be inspired with these prayers.

I pray with Your thanks and guidance
that this book reach in some little way
every individual that it needs to reach
to inspire and assist them in their struggles
and that they can come to know
You are simply just a whisper away.

As I look to the months and days ahead,
I pray You always continue to show me
the way out of the darkness and into the light
and that in my heart and soul
I will come to feel safe and normal as I once felt.

I thank You for helping me
to see Your love has no limits and no boundaries
and Your strength surpasses all fears
on whatever journey I need to take.

I thank You for touching me as You have
and for showing me I am safe with You.

With much love and light, I've come into this world
and with much love and light I shall leave.

I thank You for Your love and light that guides me
and for Christ, Michael the Archangel, Mother Mary
and all guides assisting me on my path.

I thank You for giving me such beautiful gifts
of kindness, empathy and understanding.
Amen

Chapter Twenty-Four
WHAT PRAYER CAN DO

I want to write about death and dying.
There is a part of us that fears living
and in that fear of living, we also fear dying.

This past year I've faced death quite a lot
which has terrified me and rocked me to my very soul.

And yet, it has also helped me identify
those who are important in my life,
and those who care and have been there for me.

In facing death, I have come to recognize
that there are so many things
I would go back and change about my life if I could.

Yet, in the past eight months, I have received
a great deal more insight into God,
guides, healing and believing
there is a higher power.

What has been most important as
I have come to see is that often when a healing miracle
does happen,
I don't recognize it.
It happens without my even knowing it,
which is rather strange and ironic,
because it is natural to look for immediate proof.

Yet, I realize when God heals,
God rarely takes credit for anything.
It just happens. It just is. It's just there.

We might rationalize it as something other than God
that has healed us or has guided us.

In discussing death, I realize that a part of the fear
is believing that we will be abandoned in life.
When our loved ones leave, we are left alone.

Whether facing death, or being a successor,
or even sickness,
it's a lot to process because either way
we face abandonment and being alone.

Is it any wonder why we fear being sick?
Perhaps why COVID is so dominant in our attention
is that we fear it as death
and that death may be stronger than we are.

I wonder if we would be as fearful
if we were more aware of the options with prayer,
God and believing in a heaven we do not know exists.

If more of us paint with God
and realize that God is there to help us express ourselves,
to walk with us and to show us our path,
would there be any fear left?

If we learn to speak with God
and pray with God each day,
much of our fear will leave us
before our time to face death.

I still have fears
but is it really death I fear,
or is it God, my own success or my own destiny
that I have come to fulfill in this lifetime?

We come to face our fears and all the demons
we create and perceive
as trying to possess us in a lifetime.

So, I encourage you to paint with God,
and dance with the angels,
the archangels and the Dancing Angels who heal.

Find guides and angels who will help you to heal
and heal those around you
to change your life dramatically.

Our mission in life as messengers of God
is to find that message within
and deliver it to those around us.

Become a messenger of God,
of love, of light, of healing
and come to find your true purpose.

Chapter Twenty-Five
HELP ME TO BELIEVE PRAYER

My prayer is:

*Dear God,
Help me to see and believe in myself,
and to see and believe in who You are
and why You assist me in the way You do.*

*I pray You create miracles with me and You teach me how to heal.
I pray this miracle comes with You healing me.*

*Open the door of healing
from heaven and from within where You reside
and allow me to heal quickly and easily
and to trust myself in the choices and decisions
I make regarding my health and healing.*

*Show me You are with me constantly,
helping me to breathe and to heal,
to see, to hear, to know
and to trust my intuition.
Show me a healthier way of living
with more nourishing foods.*

*Give me strength through Your love.
Help me to see the world through Your eyes,
to see those who are less fortunate
and those who are more fortunate,
and to distinguish the difference.*

*Show me how to be kinder and more charitable to others and to help those who are in need,
whether it is family, friends and loved ones who are near or far.*

Show me compassion and empathy
and how to teach others in my life
compassion and empathy.
Help me in refining all my senses
and to heal them in whatever way
they need to be healed.

Direct me on my path to the places
that I need to travel in my life.

Help me to forgive those who I believe have
wronged me
and surround them with Your healing light and love
to help them resolve their challenges and difficulties
with ease.

Help me to move on with my life
to find much greater health and happiness
with Your light.
Amen

Chapter Twenty-Six
SPIRITUAL DEVELOPMENT

It's time to discuss
what exactly spiritual development is all about.

When I look back over the years,
my spiritual development has been very much
about becoming aware, maturing,
looking at others, looking at myself
and coming to understand not everyone is the same.

We all think differently. We feel differently.
God has given all of us many different gifts
and I had the good fortune over the years
to learn and to tap in with gifts
I never realized I had before.

This book has helped me to realize
that as you develop and grow spiritually,
your intuition helps you become aware
of not only others' challenges and difficulties
but their assets and their capabilities as well.

Everyone becomes a mirror for you.
When we don't like someone,
there is probably something we don't like about ourselves.
What we find attractive in another is usually something
we really like about ourselves or wish to develop more of.

Seeing everyone as a mirror
can make life appear to be tougher
when you see the different sides of yourself
through other people.

Every person is a part of that bigger puzzle
that is called God.
We are all a part of God.

I've had good fortune over the years in developing
my intuition.

I've met a lot of wonderful people.
I've grown with them, and they've shown me things
and helped me to develop more fully
than I would have on my own.

Many might assume that to develop psychic and intuitive
abilities it requires constant meditation.
In my own experience,
nothing could be further from the truth.
All I've ever done
was to just "really want" to develop.

I talked to my spirit guides and with God.
And the more I talked,
and the more questions I asked,
the more I developed spiritually,
and the stronger my awareness became.

If you really want to tap your Kundalini,
what I would simply say is be aware it is not a free ticket.
You're not going to tap it
and then be able to say, oh I can heal myself and everything
is wonderful.
That's not how it works.
If you tap the Kundalini, there is a price tag,
and that price tag could be being sick or anxiety ridden
for months,
which in some circumstances may need to be paid
right up front.

When you do start to tap your Kundalini,
it also moves the energy through the body and
removes blocks that one may have emotionally and
otherwise.
If there is a traumatic past
or where you've been traumatized in your youth,
then that is something the Kundalini will work on to
help you heal.
Sometimes, it helps to heal creative blocks, to listen,
to see and so forth.

What I would say is
if your intention to tap the Kundalini is for you to grow spiritually,
then by all means choose that path.
But keep in mind it does have a price tag and it's a huge one.

I leave you with this prayer and affirmation.
Utilize these for comfort whenever you choose.

Prayer:

Dear God,
I come to You in search of myself,
in search of my soul,
of understanding and accepting myself
and seeing with greater depth who I am.

I desire to also know You better.
Assist me to be more intuitive,
to ignite my healing energy
and to help myself with healing
and assist others in their healing.

I thank You God for all that has come my way
and especially for this opportunity,
as I know I will grow and learn greatly.
Amen

Affirmation:

In God, I trust and know
that I am protected, loved,
accepted and embraced by angels.

I am safe and free in God's loving light.

Chapter Twenty-Seven
HIGHLIGHTS OF MY SPIRITUAL DEVELOPMENT

Looking over my years of developing spiritually,
the highlight has been the period
where I've connected most with God
and with painting and music
in the past few years.
Everything I've done creatively with God
has been a highlight and an inspiration
and will continue to be in the future.

Looking ahead, I can clearly see that
developing my healing energy from within
and more strongly is certainly going to take time
and patience.
Yet, it will be incredibly worthwhile.

Developing my Kundalini energy
has taught me a great deal of patience and calm.
It's taught me to be more aware of God,
more aware of my friends' needs
and just small things I have overlooked in past.

In writing this book, I've also learned a phenomenal amount.
I've also gained a greater respect for writers
and people in the spiritual field helping others.

I have become more conscious
of giving to others who are in need
and assisting those who God believes
need my help.

I have become a greater participant in my life
instead of standing back and observing.

I am participating and conscious of my journey
from moment to moment and day to day.

It takes a great deal of work and focus to be in the moment,
aware of my guides in the moment
and aware of God in the moment.

As I look forward to the weeks and the months ahead,
I'm sure God will guide me towards my hopes
and expectations.

God's gift to me in the past eight months has been a greater
awareness of my life, my needs and those who are
close to me.
If you are working with people
and helping them to heal on their path,
the most important gift you can give them
is honesty, truth and awareness.

Be aware of what others need,
but don't just be aware,
also be there giving them honest and truthful feedback
to the things they need to know or want to know.
Help them by giving them honest, insightful information
that is going to move them forward.

Developing intuitively and spiritually
is the greatest challenge
you can set for yourself in your life.

You will look at every part of your life,
from your health to your beliefs, to your awareness,
your thoughts, your expressions to God,
your family, your friends and your loved ones.

If you wish to develop your connection with God,
start by simply talking to God and saying:

> *"God, I want to know who You are,*
> *how You are in my life,*
> *how You reside in my life*
> *and to know You are here".*

You're asking for a kaleidoscope
of experiences and wonderment
because God is just so many different things

and it will certainly broaden your horizon and scope
beyond your comprehension.

In this great puzzle called life
that we all partake in,
we need to stand back and ask ourselves:
Where do we fit into this puzzle?
How do we make the puzzle complete?
What is it we are here to do?
And the answer could be so many different things.

One could be here to simply be charitable,
working to give to others and sacrificing.
If you are not sacrificing, you are not giving.

Life in a big city can harden one into a rat race
of searching for material gratification,
the best-looking friends and the best of everything.

The unfortunate part is one can lose oneself so easily,
looking for the outer
and forgetting to look for the inner.

I pray that you look to the inner,
the beautiful part of yourself
and that you may always continue to see it.

May you always be open to God
and allow yourself to express
who you really are
and to love what you see.

I leave you with this thought,
my go-to thought when I feel alone,
or just out for a day's hike:

> *God is with me wherever I go.*
> *I am constantly in His light and always safe.*
> *The life I live with God is full of love, light, joy,*
> *happiness and inspiration.*

I pray that you find God,
if that is what you choose.

About the Author

Spiritual Author, Painter and Musician

Adrian Keats is a Canadian spiritual author, teacher and artist currently residing in Toronto. Born February 27, 1958 in Newcastle, New Brunswick, Canada, Adrian lived all of his childhood years in the Maritimes. In 1981, he moved to Toronto and embarked on a career as a spiritual advisor.

He spent his life dedicated to his spiritual growth, development of his intuitive and psychic abilities as well as many avenues of creative expression. Adrian has taught classes, lectured on speaking with spirit, obtained psychic abilities and perhaps most importantly in recent years, helped others with their awareness of their own inner light, healing abilities and opportunities to speak with God. Adrian presently teaches classes on energy, intuition and spiritual self-development, and writes spiritual books.

Adrian always had a desire to be creative but that would take years to manifest in painting and music. Writing has always been a passion since the early eighties but only in the past couple of years has he devoted time to writing songs and creating melodies. Adrian's debut album was released in late 2020. His songs can be found on iTunes, Spotify and YouTube featuring songs such as 'Running with the Devil', 'Superman Kissed Me' and 'I'm a Cowboy in My Dreams'.

Websites: www.adriankeats.com
www.paintingwithgod.world

Email: info@adriankeats.com

Phone: 647-772-3958 (Canada)

Manufactured by Amazon.ca
Bolton, ON

28477771R00085